I0114790

Weather-Magic in Inner Asia

Indiana University Uralic and Altaic Series
Denis Sinor, Editor
Volume 158

WEATHER-MAGIC IN INNER ASIA

BY

ÁDÁM MOLNÁR

With an Appendix
Alttürkische Fragmente über den Regenstein
by
P. Zieme

Indiana University
Research Institute for Inner Asian Studies
Bloomington, Indiana
1994

Library of Congress Catalog Card Number: 94-69065
ISBN: 0-933070-33-0

Printed in the United States of America

CONTENTS

ABBREVIATIONS

Abušqa	Chaghatai, see Véliaminov-Zernov 1869
Aks.	Ottoman Turkish, see *Tarama Sözlüğü*
Alt.	Altai Turkic
Atai.H.	Ottoman Turkish, see *Tarama Sözlüğü*
ATu.	Ancient Turkic
Av.	Avestan
Az.	Azeri
Bur.	Buriat
Bashk.	Bashkir
Chuv	Chuvash
CrimT	Crimean Tatar
Chagh.	Chaghatai
Damaskin	Manuscript, see Kononov 1972, pp. 89—92.
ETurki	Eastern Turki, the same as "New Uighur"
Gag.	Gagauz
IIr.	Indo-Iranian
Ir.	Iranian
Kalm.	Kalmuck
Kar.	Karaim
Kashgh.	Khakani, Kāshgharī
Kaz.	Kazak
KazT	Kazan Tatar
Kh.	Khalkha
Khot.	Khotani Saka
Kirgh.	Kirghiz
Kurd.	Kurdish
LMo.	Literary Mongolian
LughT.	Chaghatai, see Pavet de Courteille 1870.
M	stands for 'motive'
MIK III 192	see Appendix
MIr.	Middle Iranian
MMo.	Middle Mongolian
Mo.	Mongolian

MPe.	Middle Persian
MTu.	Middle Turkic
Oir.	Oirat
OIr.	Old Iranian
Ott.	Ottoman Turkish
OTu.	Old Turkic
NIr.	New Iranian
NPe.	New Persian
NTu.	New Turkic
Pe.	Persian
Sanglakh	Chaghatai, see Clauson 1960
SHM	*The Secret History of the Mongols* see Haenisch 1962
Skt.	Sanskrit
Sogd.	Sogdian
T III S 501	(*U 3004*) see Appendix
TobolT	Tobol Tatar
Torma	Bashkir, quoted from J. Torma's unpublished material
Trkm.	Turkmen
TT IV	see Bang—Gabain 1930
TT X	see Gabain 1958
Tu.	Turkic
Tuv.	Tuvinian
U II	see Müller 1910
Uigh.	Uighur
Uzb.	Uzbek
Yak.	Yakut
YUigh.	Yellow Uighur

FIGURES

Maps

KEY TO THE SYMBOLS USED

/ /	encloses a phonemic transcription
[ ]	encloses a phonetic transcription
<>	encloses a letter
>	"becomes" in historical linguistics
<	"comes from" in historical linguistics
*	marks a reconstructed earlier form
→	borrowed from
△	man
○	woman
△ | △	father and son
=	marriage
⇒	implies
+	presence
−	absence
∧	and

INTRODUCTION

The present book deals with weather-magic, a major constituent of Inner Asian Turkic and Mongol natural religion. The rather general term "natural religion" (the term "belief-system" would be a synonym) covers all the genuinely religious notions, beliefs, cults and rites of the Turks and the Mongols. The term "natural religion" has been accepted in the most recent and comprehensive handbook of Inner Asian history, (ed. Sinor) *The Cambridge History of Early Inner Asia*, (see Index, p. 511). Among other names used for this belief-sytem, the most popular is "shamanism".[1] A sub-system of Turkic and Mongol animism, the cult of heaven, is often termed "Tengrism".[2] Weather-magic is a particular type of magic, a structured set of beliefs and the rites connected to them, rites aimed at effecting changes in the weather.[3] The main emphasis of this study will be limited to Inner Asian Turkic weather-magic. However, Turkic and Mongol religious notions have become so intimately connected that one cannot be understood without the other.

Ever since Hammer-Purgstall's pioneering philological and historical work published in 1840[4] called attention to Turkic and Mongol weather-magic, scholars have discovered it to be a topic that occurs in sources dealing with the Turks and the Mongols with surprising frequency. Quatremère[5], in a note written to his edition of Rashīd al-Dīn's *Jāmi ' al-Tawārīkh*, gave an extensive catalog of the Islamic sources dealing with the subject, supplementing it with a list of accounts by thirteenth-century and later European travellers. Quatremère's footnote remains perhaps the

---

[1] See *e.g.* Malov 1947, Boyle 1972, Potapov 1978, etc.

[2] The *terminus technicus* was coined by Roux 1956—1957, p. 206.

[3] Frazer 1911, pp. 247—331.

[4] 1840, p. 15, note 1, p. 42, 206, note 1 and pp. 435-38.

[5] 1836, pp. 428—40.

most comprehensive overview of the Islamic sources on Turkic and Mongol weather-magic. Still, in the last century, Andrian[6] supplemented the Islamic sources with the evidence of ethnographical observations made by his contemporaries. Unfortunately, however, he confused the rain-stone (Mo. *ǰada*, Tu. *yada*) with the jade, and this mistake led him to draw some equally mistaken conclusions.

In this century, Mongol weather-magic was first discussed by Yule[7]; and a few years later, Köprülü Zade[8] clarified several philological aspects of the Islamic sources on Turkic weather-magic. In several of his works Pelliot[9] noted that the rain-stone was not to be confused with the jade. Collections of sources were published by Turkish scholars - valuable fresh material including both formerly unedited Islamic sources[10] and ethnographical data[11]. Doerfer's contribution[12] was to treat the linguistic aspect of the subject. The most detailed philological investigation of the historical sources on Turkic and Mongol weather-magic was carried out by Roux[13] and Boyle.[14]

For my part, I have aimed at combining the historical, the philological-linguistic and the ethnographical approaches. The written historical records will be discussed in Chapter 1, the anthropological data in Chapter 2, and the linguistic arguments in Chapter 3. In Chapter 4, an attempt will be made to identify and define the types of beliefs and rites involved in weather-magic, and to trace their historical development.

---

[6] 1893.

[7] 1921, i, pp. 309–11, note 8.

[8] 1925.

[9] 1949, pp. 8–9, note 3; 1959–1963–1973, i, pp. 424–5.

[10] Yaltkaya 1943, pp. 693–8.

[11] Inan 1954, pp. 160–4; Tanyu 1968, pp. 41–72 Oğuz 1980, ii, pp. 954–95 and Şeşen 1981, p. 64.

[12] 1963, pp. 286–9.

[13] 1958a, pp. 449–51, 1984, pp. 95–8; and 1984, pp. 95–98.

[14] 1972, pp. 184-91.

Chapter 5 will deal with the role played by weather-magic and its practitioners in Inner Asian nomadic societies.

In the course of writing this book, I repeatedly found myself having to trespass on areas beyond the rather narrow limits of my competence as a Turkologist. I had the good fortune, however, of receiving generous help from a number of specialists. Peter Zieme (Berlin), has contributed an Appendix, *Alttürkische Fragmente über den Regenstein;* the two fragments in the Turfan-collection which he has discovered appear for the first time in this volume. István Zimonyi (Szeged) has translated from Arabic originals several passages so far not available in Western languages, and offered his help with their philological and textual interpretation. Nicholas Sims-Williams (School of Oriental and African Studies, University of London) has made useful suggestions and corrections in the Iranological part of Chapter 3. The entire manuscript has been read by György Kara and Katalin U. Kőhalmi (Budapest), who made a number of corrections and additions, mostly in the parts impinging on Mongol philology and anthropology. My thanks are also due to Zsuzsanna Draskovits (Budapest), who designed the maps.

WEATHER-MAGIC IN HISTORICAL RECORDS

THE PRE-TÜRK PERIOD

The first mention of weather-magic in Inner Asia is in the *Wei shu*[1], in connection with the Yüeh-pan. The Yüeh-pan tribe of Hsiung-nu origin settled on the northern slopes of the T'ien-shan at the end of the first century.[2] In the middle of the fifth century[3] the Yüeh-pan are located northwest of the Tarbaghatai Mountains and of the Ili River; they are spoken of as the western neighbours of the Juan-juan with whom they had initially friendly, and later hostile relations. The *Wei shu* relates, that in the state of the Yüeh-pan there are magicians who, when the Yüeh-pan are attacked by the Juan-juan, are able to conjure protracted periods of rain, strong winds and floods. As shall be seen in Chapter 4, the fact that the Yüeh-pan were located in the region of the Ili River and the Tarbaghatai Mountains is of special importance from the point of view of the history of weather-magic.

In the seventh century, another type of weather-magic is reported by the *T'ang shu* in the description of K'ang-chü: in the eleventh month of the year, the natives of that country hoped for cold weather with drums and dances, and entertained themselves by sprinkling water on each other. In Kucha, a similar rite was common in T'ang times: people threw water at each other and spilled it on the ground in front of their houses in the period lasting from the first to the seventh day of the seventh month

---

[1] Bichurin 1950—53, ii, p. 260.

[2] Czeglédy 1983, p. 102.

[3] Pelliot 1903, p. 100.

according to the lunar calendar.[4] The Chinese traveller, Wang Yen-te, who visited the Turfan region in the 980s, also described a local, presumably Iranian, rite in the Turfan Basin: the natives filled silver and copper tubes with water, and amused themselves with sprinkling each other. It was, as Wang Yen-te noted, their way to beat the heat, and prevent diseases.[5]

THE TÜRKS

Turkic weather-magic first appears in one of the ancestral legends of the Türks.[6] The *Chou shu* (50, 2a), compiled around A.D.629, relates that the ancestor of the Türks originated from the country of So, located north of the Hsiung-nu. The chief of this tribe was A-pang-pu, who had seventy brothers. One, called I-chih-ni-shi-tu, was born of a she-wolf. A-pang-pu and his brothers were slow-witted, so their country was soon destroyed. (I-chih)-ni-shi-tu had the supernatural power to produce wind and rain. He had two wives, daughters of the Spirit of the Summer and the Spirit of the Winter. Both A-pang-pu and I-chih-ni-shi-tu are legendary figures, and the precise location of the country of So is uncertain. In any case, I-chih-ni-shi-tu had four sons by one of his wives; one of them established the state of the Ch'i-ku (Kirghiz) between the rivers A-fu (Abakan) and Chien (Käm), while another founded the realm of the T'u-chüeh (Türk).

Less than two decades after the compilation of the *Chou shu*, we find the same magical power of the Turks related at the other end of the Turkic world. A fragmentary, anonymous Syriac chronicle records that Elias, the metropolitan of Marv, travelled to the frontiers of Marv in c.644, where he baptized a local Turkic ruler. He convinced the reluctant king of the might of God by stopping the winds and storms that had been

---

[4] See Malyavkin 1974, p. 168, note 764.

[5] Julien 1847, pp. 57–8.

[6] Liu 1958,i, pp. 5–6; Sinor 1982, pp. 226–30.

summoned by the sorcerers of the Turks.[7] The date (644) and the location (East of Marv) allows the supposition that the Metropolitan Elias met and baptized one of the petty Turkic rulers who had been vassals of the Western Türk Empire.[8]

A CONSPECTUS OF THE EARLY ISLAMIC SOURCES

Early Islamic sources show that rituals in which stones were used to change the weather seemed curious to the Arabs, who had their own, different, practices of weather-magic.[9] Though scepticism as to the efficacy of these rites is clearly discernible in the accounts of the Islamic authors, they must be credited for their attempts to fit these phenomena into the framework of everything else they knew about the Turks. At first

---

[7] "Elias autem metropolita urbis Marū (*Marw*) permultos e Turcis aliisque gentibus ad fidem convertit; Marū autem flumen est de cuius nomine urbs et regio nomen acceperunt... De Elia isto metropolita urbis Marū narrant haec: cum peragraret loca quae ad fines exteriores ex interiore parte sunt, regulus quidam ei obviam fuit qui ad bellum cum alio rege gereudum iter faciebat. A quo cum multum expetisset Elias ut bello desisteret, respondit ille se Dei eius, *Eliae*, cultum susceptureum, dummodo Elias miracula ostenderet, qualia sacerdotes deorum quos ipse colebat ostendebant. *Iussu autem reguli, sacerdotes daemonum cultores qui eum comitabantur, daemones quibus serviebant invocaverunt, et confestim aer obscuratus est nubibus, dum venti et tonitrua et fulgara sine intermissione ingruunt. Tunc divina vi commotus Elias caelesti cruce se signavit, et quam daemones rebelles congesserant hallucinationem cohibuit, quae subito omnino evanuit. Tunc regulus, visis quae sanctus Elias patraverat, pronus veneratus est, et cum suo comitatu fidem *christianam* amplexus est. Ad flumen quoddam eos deduxit *Elias*, atque ad unum baptizavit, tum sacerdotibus et diaconis constitutis in suam regionem reversus est." Guidi 1903, pp. 28, 29).

[8] Nöldeke 1893, pp. 39–40; Brockelmann 1925, p. 111.

[9] Fahd 1978.

glance, it seems that all relevant references in the writings of the early Arab and Persian writers can be traced to one of five traditions:

i. The story of the rain-stone in the mountain pass in the land of the Karluks. The most detailed discussion of this tradition is by Yaltkaya[10], based partly on unedited manuscripts kept in Istanbul. The story first occurs in the *Kitāb al-Khawwāṣṣ al-Kabīr*, "The Great Book of Attributes", ascribed to Jābir Ibn Ḥayyān, the great Arabic scholar of the eighth century A.D.[11]

The rain-stones in the valley of the Karluks were also mentioned by another important figure of classical Arabic scholarship, Muḥammad ibn Zakariyyā' al-Rāzī (865—925), in his lost *Kitāb al-Khawwāṣṣ*.[12] The relevant passage is quoted by Abu'l-Rayḥān Muḥammad ibn Aḥmad al-Bīrūnī (973—c.1050) in his treatise on mineralogy, the *Kitāb al-Jamāhir fī Ma'rifat al-Jawāhir* "The Compilation of All Knowledge on Precious Stones", written under the reign of Sultān Mawdūd ibn Mas'ūd (1041—49).[13] According to Yaltkaya[14], the relevant passage from al-Rāzī's *Kitāb al-Khawwāṣṣ* has also survived in Nāṣir al-Dīn Ṭūsī's treatise on mineralogy and precious stones, the *Tansuqnāma-i Ilkhānī*.[15]

The rain-stones in the valley of the Karluks are mentioned in later Arab works as well, such as Pseudo-Majrītī's *Kitāb Ghāyat al-Ḥakīm*, "The Aim of the Sage", compiled after A.D.1051.[16] It is interesting to note that the rain-stones in the valley of the Karluks were not unknown to medieval Europeans, thanks to translations of this work into Latin and

---

[10] 1943, pp. 693—8.

[11] Yaltkaya (1943, p. 694) gives the Turkish translation of the same text, based on Jābir's *Kitāb al-Baḥth* "The Book of Research" (Istanbul, Veliyiddin Efendi Kütüphanesi, S. 56—75, No. 2564); see also Kraus 1942—43, ii, p. 75—76, note 1.

[12] Kraus 1942—43, i, LXI—LXII and ii. p. 63, note 5.

[13] Boilot 1960, p. 1236.

[14] *Op. cit.*, p. 694.

[15] On the unedited Mss. of this work, see Ullmann 1972, p. 127, note 3.

[16] Ritter—Plessner 1962, p. 397.

other European languages (*e.g.* into Spanish in 1256)[17]. Finally, ibn Khaldūn (1332—1406) likewise touched upon the magicians in the country of the Turks who could produce rain.[18]

ii. The origin of the rain-stone from the mountains of the east. An Islamized tradition on the origin of the rain-stone has been preserved in Yāqūt[19] al-Rūmī's *Mu'jam al-Buldān*, "A Dictionary of Countries" under the item "Turkistan". Yāqūt refers to Aḥmad ibn Muḥammad ibn Isḥāq ibn al-Faqīh al-Hamadhānī who, in turn, names Abū-l-'Abbās 'Īsā ibn Muḥammad al-Marwazī as his source. According to al-Nadīm's *Fihrist*[20], Ja'far ibn Aḥmad al-Marwazī, surnamed Abū al-'Abbās, wrote about the sciences. He was the first to write a book about roads and kingdoms, but before he could complete this work, death overtook him, shortly before 887/88. Marwazī's informant was Dāwud ibn Manṣur ibn Abī 'Alī al-Badhghīsī, the governor of Khurāsān who, in turn, had heard the story of the rain-stone from an Oghuz prince named Balqīq ibn Jabbūya[21].

Yāqūt's *Dictionary* has preserved the narrative in its most complete form, while in the existing copies of his source, Ibn al-Faqīh's *Kitāb al-Buldān*, "A Book of Countries", there is only a short summary on the pebbles of the Turks, stones they are said to have wrested from some animals in the countries of the East.[22] There is one addition to this

[17] Ullmann 1972, p. 385.

[18] Fahd 1966, p. 187.

[19] 1979, ii, pp. 24—6.

[20] Dodge 1970, i, p. 329.

[21] Yāqūt (*op. cit.*, ii, p. 25) gives al-Qīq ibn Ḥaywayah. A Turkic name can be expected here, it seems that al-Qīq ibn Ḥaywayah is a corrupted pseudo-Arabic form of Balqīq ibn Jabbūya as suggested by Togan (1948, p. 15) and Pritsak (1951, p. 405).

[22] Goeje 1885, pp. 329—30.

summary in the Mashhad manuscript of Ibn al-Faqīh's work that was discovered by Togan in 1923.[23]

iii. The rivalry for the rain-stone among the sons of Japheth. The narrative on the origin of the rain-stone among the Turks is told by Abū Sa'īd 'Abd al-Ḥayy ibn Ḍaḥḥāk Gardīzī in his *Zayn al-Akhbār* "Jewel of Narratives", written in 1050. He gives as his source Abū 'Amr 'Abdullāh ibnu-'l-Muqaffa''s (720—c.757) work the *Rub' al-Dunyā*, "The [Habitable] Quarters of the World". However, Czeglédy[24] argues that Gardīzī's chapter on the Turks relates events that took place between 745 and 760—766. Consequently, it must have been written not by Muqaffa' himself, but by his son, who embarked on his literary career after 780, or more probably, by some unknown Persian author. Be that as it may, the story should be dated to the second half of the eighth century.[25]

The same story of the origin of the Turks and the rain-stone is recounted in a somewhat different way with a non-identical set of eponymous heroes by the unknown author of the *Mujmal al-Tawārīkh wa 'l-Qiṣaṣ* "Digest of Chronicles and Narratives" written in 1126.[26]

iv. Tamīm ibn Baḥr's account of the pebbles of the Toquzoghuz kings. Tamīm ibn Baḥr's account occurs frequently in Islamic sources, both with and without credit of his authorship. Tamīm ibn Baḥr provides us with first-hand information acquired during his journey he made to the capital of the Uighurs in 821.[27] His account was included in ibn Khurdādhbih's *Kitāb al-masālik wa 'l-mamālik*, "The Book of Roads and Kingdoms", and was copied by Ibn al-Faqīh who gives a condensed form

---

[23] Togan reported on this manuscript in 1924 (under the name Validov) and in 1948.

[24] 1973, pp. 260—7.

[25] Gardīzī is cited after Martinez 1982, pp. 116—7.

[26] Bahār (ed.) 1318/1939.

[27] Minorsky 1948.

of the story on the rain-stone of the Toquzoghuz kings.[28] Thus, in Ibn al-Faqīh's *Kitāb al-Buldān* we find the digest of three traditions, namely, Tamīm ibn Baḥr's account, the origin of the rain-stone among the mountains of the East, and Ismā'īl ibn Aḥmad's narrative. Yāqūt[29] also inserted, without mentioning his source, Tamīm ibn Baḥr's report before giving the story of the eastern origin of the rain-stone.

In Yāqūt's *Mu'jam al-Buldān*, under the item "Ṣīn"[30], Abū Dulaf mentions the rain-magnet (*maghnāṭīs al-maṭar*) of the Kimäks, but this hint is also ultimately derived from Tamīm ibn Baḥr's account, and most probably it referred to the Toquzoghuz, the people mentioned third after the Kimäks and the Ghuzz in Abū Dulaf's enumeration of the Turkic tribes[31]. Similarly, al-Muṭahhar ibn Ṭāhir al-Maqdisī, who touches upon the magical skill that some Turks have of conjuring up snow, wind and hail[32], had drawn upon Tamīm ibn Baḥr. Finally, Andrian[33] quotes Zakariyyā' ibn Muḥammad Abū Yaḥyā al-Qazwīnī[34], who also simply copied Abū Dulaf as found in Yāqūt's *Mu'jam al-Buldān*, without adding anything to his source.

v. The Sāmānid amīr, Ismā'īl ibn Aḥmad's narrative. The narrative can be connected to real historical events that took place during the reign of the Sāmānid ruler, Ismā'īl ibn Aḥmad (892—907). It has survived in Yāqūt's *Mu'jam al-Buldān*[35]. In this work, Yāqūt refers again to al-Marwazī, but this is undoubtedly a mistake, as Marwazī died c.886/7, that is, before Ismā'īl ibn Aḥmad's reign. In fact, Yāqūt must

---

28 Goeje 1885, pp. 329—30.

29 *Op. cit.*, ii, p. 24.

30 *Op. cit.*, iii, p. 442.

31 Consequently, all references to the weather-magic of the Kimäks (Yule 1921, i, p. 309, note 8; Şeşen 1981, p. 64, etc.) are erroneous.

32 Huart 1899—1919, xviii, p. 22.

33 1893, pp. 58—9.

34 Wüstenfeld 1848—9, i, p. 395; on Qazwīnī see Ruska 1913, pp. 18—33.

35 *Op. cit.*, ii, pp. 25—26.

have derived the account from Ibn al-Faqīh's *Kitāb al-Buldān*, though it is only the skeleton of the story that we find in Ibn al-Faqīh.[36]

THE UIGHURS

As with the Türks, weather-magic among the Uighurs is mentioned in a variety of sources. Uighur magicians are mentioned by the *Chiu T'ang shu* in connection with a campaign against the Tibetans in which they were allies of T'ang forces:

> Before this, Po Yüan-kuang and others had gone west of Ling-t'ai Subprefecture [1/11/765?] to ascertain how powerful the robbers were. Because the moon was bright, they thought that it would be better if it were darker, so the Uighurs got some magicians opportunely to call up wind and snow. At dawn there was a battle [2/11/765?]. All the Tibetans were bitterly cold and freezing. Their bows and arrows were all useless, they had wrapped themselves in felt and were slowly moving forward. Yüan-kuang and the Uighurs followed and killed them, covering the plains [with their corpses].[37]

A Muslim traveller, Tamīm ibn Baḥr Muṭṭawwi'i, who in 821 visited Qarabalghasun, the Uighur capital on the Orkhon, provides first-hand information which fully corroborates the *Chiu T'ang shu*:

[36] Goeje 1885, pp. 329–30.

[37] Mackerras 1972, p. 82.

> And of the wonders of the country of the Turks are some pebbles they have, with which they bring down rain, snow, cold, etc., as they wish. The story of these pebbles in their possession is well known and widely spread and no Turk denies it. And these (pebbles) are especially in the possession of the king of the Toghuzghuz[38] and no other of their kings possesses them.[39]

The Arabic source complements the Chinese. While the *Chiu T'ang shu* tells about the use by the Uighurs of weather-magic in warfare, the Arabic author reveals that it was performed by means of certain "pebbles".

The Karluks and the Islamic Legends on the Origin of the Rain-Stone among the Turks

Concerning the origin of the rain-stone among the Turks, two legends have been recorded by Islamic writers. Explicitly or implicitly, the Karluks play a central role in both of them. In the first, the rain-stone appears in the Islamic ancestral legend of the Turks, which is given in its most extensive form by Gardīzī:

> [However] in his book on *The [Habitable] Quarter of the World,* Abū-'Amr-e 'Abdo-'llah Ebno-'l Moqaffa' (Ibnu'l-Muqaffa') states that when the prophet Noah, upon whom be peace, came out from the ark, the world had become devoid of people. He had three sons, [to wit] Shem, Ham and Japheth, and he divided the earth among

---

[38] *I. e.* the Uighur.

[39] Minorsky 1948, p. 285, Arabic text p. 282.

his sons. The Land of the Blacks, such as Azania *(Zanj)*, Abyssinia, Nubia, Barbary and *Phazania *(wa*<Fazz>ān)*, and the maritime and [southern] region of Persia *(wa deyār-e barr-o-baḥr o ḥeiyez-e Īrān)* he gave to Ham; 'Iraq, Xorāsān. Ḥejāz, Yemen, Syria and the Iranian Realm *(Īrān-Šahr)* became the portion of Shem; [while the lands of] the Turks, the Saqlābs, and [the tribes of] Gog and Magog as far as China fell to Japheth. In as much as these lands of Turkestan were (the) farthest away from the areas of cultivation *(ābādānī) he named them "Tark"* (*i.e.* "abandonment; neglected land fallen from cultivation"). [Accordingly,] Noah, upon whom be peace, prayed and entreated the Lord, Almighty and Glorious, that He might teach Japheth a Name [of His], which when he called [upon Him by] it, rain would at once come, and the Lord, Almighty and Glorious, at once hearkened unto that prayer and [so] taught Japheth.

[Now,] when Japheth learned that Name, he wrote it on a stone [which] he suspended about his neck out of precaution, lest he should forget it. [Thereafter,] whenever he craved for rain [by that Name,] it would rain. [Moreover,] if he were to touch that stone to water and give that water to a sick person, [that person] would become better. That stone his descendants continued to hold as their inheritance until his progeny, such as the Ǧuzz, the Xallux, the Xazar, and the likes of them, became too many, at which time contention arose among them because of that stone.

[At that time] the stone was in the hands of the Ǧuzz and they agreed that on such and such a day [all the tribes] would come together, and cast lots to see whose lot that stone would fall, to whom [then] they would give it. [However,] the Ǧuzz took another stone that was exactly

> alike in shape (*ham bar ān meθāl*) and inscribed that prayer on it, and that counterfeit stone their chief hung about his neck. Then when they cast their lots on the appointed day and it fell to the Xallux, they gave the Xallux that falsified stone, while the original stone stayed with the Ğuzz. This is why when the Turks want rain they fashion themselves a [special] stone (*wa Torkān ke bārān x^vāhand *sang az īn sabab rāst-<konand> pro, be sang az īn sabab rāst*).[40]

This fascinating story, which attempts to fit the Turks and their lineage into the framework of the Islamic world-view, is composed of motifs of various origin. That of the father distributing his realm among his sons is a well-known *topos*. Since Gardīzī's work forms part and parcel of Persian historiography, it is, perhaps, enough to refer here to the Iranian national tradition according to which Frēdōn divided his world empire among his three sons. The two elder brothers, Salm and Tūr, conspired to murder the youngest son, Ēraj, and thus began the interminable feud between Iran and Turan.[41]

As Gardīzī tells the story, the Turks received some arid lands as a result of Noah's apportionment; indeed, thence their name, *Turk*. The legend explains the ethnic name *Turk* in terms of the Arabic verb *taraka*, or more precisely, of its derivative, *tark* 'deserted', *i.e.* 'desert'. The rain-stone is brought into the story through a sleight of hand worked by this folk-etymology: the Turks lived in an arid land; consequently, they needed some means of producing rain. The last motif of the legend is the competition for the rain-stone among the Turkic tribes. Theoretically, all Turkic tribes take part in the contest for the stone. Gardīzī, however, names only three of them: the Ghuzz (Oghuz), the Khallukh (Karluks) and the Khazars. The real rivals are the Oghuz and the Karluks, while the

---

[40] Persian text Ḥabibi 1968, pp. 256; English translation Martinez 1982, pp. 116–7.

[41] Yarshater 1983, p. 372.

Khazars play an entirely passive role in the story. The point is that the Karluks are the lawful owners of the stone, it having been allotted to them. The Oghuz can get it only by guile. The outcome of the drawing must, clearly, be regarded as a revelation of God's will. Thus the structure of the legend can be represented as follows:

$$[M_1 \wedge M_2] \Rightarrow M_3 \Rightarrow M_4$$

Figure 1. The structure of Gardīzī's account of the origin of the Turks M_1: the father distributes his realm among his sons M_2: the folk etymology of the ethnic name Turk M_3: the idea of a rain-stone to produce rain in an arid land M_4: the rivalry for the rain-stone, which lawfully belongs to the Karluks, but which the Oghuz take by fraud.

Since the folk-etymology of the ethnic name *Turk* makes sense only in Arabic, the connection between the origin of the Turks and the rain-stone must be the result of Islamic scholarly speculation. On the other hand, the account that the Turks had rain-stones with the magical ability of producing rain emerges as a piece of authentic knowledge about the Turks on the part of Islamic scholars.

The same story is told by the anonymous author of the *Mujmal al-Tawārīkh* in a somewhat different way:

> I have read that when Noah, upon whom be peace, portioned the Earth among his sons after the Flood had ebbed, he gave all the lands on the other bank of the Jaihūn[42] to Japheth, while he gave the lands of the Arabs, the two 'Irāqs, Yemen and those regions to Shem, and Egypt, Greece, the Land of the Copts, Barbary, India and Zanzibar to Ham; the peoples of these lands are their descendants. We shall tell the tradition concerning Japheth.

[42] I. e. the Oxus, or Syr-Darya.

> As the story goes, Japheth wanted to be admitted to the presence of his father, and said, "Oh, Prophet of the Lord, the land you gave me has insufficient water, and it is desolate. Teach me a prayer, by which—whenever rain is wanted—we can call upon the Lord, may He be exalted, and gain a hearing." Noah, upon whom be peace, prayed, and the Lord, may He be honoured and glorified, revealed his own Name, and Noah taught it to his son. Japheth carved it in a stone, suspended it about his neck as an amulet, and left. Whenever he called upon the Lord by that Name in case of need, [it rained].

The *Mujmal al-Tawārīkh* then relates legendary stories about the sons of Japheth, and it returns to the rain-stone of the Turks in the story of Ghuzz, the grandson of Japheth:

> Afterwards, Ghuzz took his place of residence bordering on that of Bulghār at the place which is nowadays the land of the Ghuzz. A war broke out between him and his father's brother, Turk. The cause of the war was that when Japheth died by the Jaihūn, the stone that had been given to him by Noah, may peace be upon Him, was in the hands of Ghuzz, as it had been entrusted to him. All the sons of Japheth came together, and they all wanted [the stone] for themselves. It was decided that they would draw lots. Ghuzz, who was avaricious and deceitful, said, "Let us draw lots tomorrow!". In the same evening he counterfeited a similar stone, and he hid the original. Afterwards, they drew lots, and Turk's name was drawn. Ghuzz said, "You are worthier [of this stone than me], oh, my uncle!", and he gave him the counterfeited stone. They returned to their abodes, and hundred and twenty years thus passed.

> Ghuzz had lots of sons, the eldest was *Yabghu*[43] by name. It once happened that Turk needed rain for his lands. He took that stone, and prayed, but no rain came. Thus Turk failed, and he came to know of the deceitfulness of Ghuzz. Turk wrote a letter to Ghuzz and reproached him. But Ghuzz did not repent, and said "You are telling a lie; you have offended the Lord, and your prayer has not been answered." Turk answered "Surely, it may have been so." After that time, whenever Ghuzz needed rain, he took the stone that Noah had given to Japheth, prayers were said, and the Lord, may He be exalted, bestowed rain on them. When this was heard by Turk, he made war on them. There were skirmishes between them, hostilities broke out. *Yabghu* was killed in the war, and it thus continued, but we do not intend to tell how and where all these events happened. However, this is the reason and the essence of the hostilities and wars between the Turks and the children of Japheth. To this very day, there has been no end to the hatred and war between them, nor will there ever be.[44]

The two variants of the legend differ principally in the names of the eponymous forefathers of the Turkic tribes; in the *Mujmal al-Tawārīkh,* the opposing parties are Ghuzz and Turk. However, the author of the *Mujmal al-Tawarīkh* relates some other adventures of Turk, son of Japheth, as follows:

> Afterwards Turk roamed over all the lands of the East, till he found a place that he thought to be agreeable, and he named it *S.kūk*. [That place] is called *S.kūk* in Turkic.

---

[43] Misspelt BYĠW.

[44] Persian text in Bahār (ed.) 1318/1939, pp. 97–8 and 102–3.

> There was a small sea (*daryā*) there; its water was hot, and there were lots of springs. There was also a mountain in the neighbourhood, full of game, and it also had its own waters. Turk offered his thanks to the Lord, and settled in that place.[45]

The abode of Turk as described in the *Mujmal al-Tawārīkh*, with its warm-water lake, can be localized to the region of the Issyk Kul[46], *i.e.* within the boundaries of Karluk territory. Consequently, the story is about the Karluks, who appear in the legend under the name "Turk". We find the same reference in other Islamic sources as well (see below): as the Karluks moved to the former Western Türk territories after 745, the appellation of the former rulers of Semirechye was transferred to them. It is very probable that the garbled form *S.kūk*, the name of the place occupied by Turk, can be emended to **Isig-Köl*.[47]

	The sons of Japheth		
	the rivals		the third party
Gardīzī	Ghuzz	Karluk	Khazar
Mujmal	Ghuzz	Turk	
Mīrkhwānd	Uzz	Turk	

Figure 2. Turkic eponymous heroes vying for the rain-stone

[45] Persian text Bahār (ed.) 1318/1939, pp. 99–100.
[46] Barthold 1968, pp. 26–7.
[47] Barthold–Spuler 1978, p. 212.

The second legend found in Islamic sources[48] on the origin of the rain-stone among the Turks tells quite another story:

> News has spread among the peoples of the East that the Turks have some pebbles by means of which they can make rain and snow whenever they wish. Aḥmad ibn Muḥammad al-Hamadhānī quotes Abū-l-ʿAbbās ʿĪsā ibn Muḥammad al-Marwazī, who said: We have heard that in the country which is behind the River[49], and in other districts adjacent to the country of the infidel Turks, Ghuzz, Toghuzoghuz and Kharlukh, they[50] have kingdoms, and an important object by means of which they can do serious harm to their enemies. We have heard that when some Turks intercede for rain or use some other methods, it rains; furthermore, they can bring on hail, snow and similar things whenever they wish. We wavered between belief and disbelief [concerning this matter], until I met Dāwud ibn Manṣūr ibn Abī ʿAlī al-Badhghīsī, who was an honest man and the governor of Khurāsān; his activities there deserve praise. Once when he was alone in the company of Balqīq al-Jabbūya, the Turkic Ghuzz king's son, he asked him: "I have heard said about the Turks that they can bring forth rain and snow, whenever they wish. What do you think about it?" He answered: "The most disdained and despised of the Turks, as Allah has it, are the ones involved in this affair. What you have heard is true. There is a story about [the rain-stone] that I shall tell you.

---

[48] Yāqūt, *Muʿjam al-Buldān*, ii, pp. 24–6.

[49] *I. e.* the Oxus.

[50] *I.e.* these Turkic tribes.

One of my ancestors had quarrelled with his father who was the king at that time, and parted with him. He took companions for himself from among his freed slaves, his pages, and others who liked rambling; and he set off toward the countries of the east. [He] attacked people and hunted down all the animals that he and his companions came across. He got to the land claimed by its inhabitants to be impossible to pass beyond, as there was a mountain at that place. They told him: 'The sun rises behind this mountain; it is so very close to the earth that it scorches everything it falls upon.' He asked: 'Are there any people or animals there?' They replied: 'Yes.' He asked: 'How can they live there under the conditions which you have described?' They replied: 'As for the people, they have passages under the ground and caves in the mountains, and when the sun rises they go into them and stay there until the sun moves away from above them, and then they come out. As for the animals, they pick up stones of which they have inspired knowledge, and each animal takes a stone in its mouth and raises its head towards the heavens. The stone casts a shadow over them, and a cloud then appears and forms a screen between the animals and the sun.' My ancestor entered that country and found it to be exactly as he had been told. He and his companions attacked the animals in order to get a look at those stones and to collect them. They took as many as they could and carried them back to their own country, where they have been ever since. If they want rain, they move them but slightly, and the clouds gather and rain comes; but if they want snow and hail, they intensify the motion, and snow and hail

> come to them. This is their story. It is not their artifice, but comes from the omnipotence of God Most High."[51]

The narrative can be completed on the basis of the Mashhad manuscript of Ibn al-Faqīh's work[52], which adds that having heard Balqīq ibn Jabbūya's story on the rain-stone from Dāwud ibn Manṣūr al-Badhghīsī, 'Īsā ibn Muḥammad al-Marwazī returned to Shāsh (Tashkent), where the wise men of the town confirmed that to their knowledge, the story was true.

The second legend on the origin of the rain-stone comes from "areas adjacent to the countries of the Turks, Ghuzz, Toquzoghuz and the Karluks" and it is an account of a raid led by an Oghuz prince to "Eastern countries". However, these "Eastern countries" appear in the story in a mythical form, and here again, we find another *topos*, borrowed from the Alexander Romance, the motif of the land of the rising sun and its troglodyte inhabitants. In the hope of finding some historical correspondence to this eastern land of the rising sun, let us turn to the earliest legend in Islamic literature on the rain-stone among the Turks, namely, the story of the rain-stone in the mountain pass in the land of the Karluks.

Probably the earliest account of this story is the one attributed to Jābir ibn Ḥayyān:

> Why is it that if we take a rain-stone (*ḥajar al-maṭar*) in the summer and put it into a washtub, cover [the rain-stone] with water until the tub is filled, and then we rub the surfaces of the stones against one another the rain comes? Is this without reason? This stone—my dear friend—occurs

---

[51] Translated by I. Zimonyi.

[52] Togan 1948, pp. 15–6. In the Mashhad Ms., the rain-stone is handed down to the Turks by Abraham and his concubine, Qanṭūrā'.

in a valley in the land of the Karluks [*khazluj*], in the part of the valley where the diamonds whose description we have presented at the beginning of this treatise, the *[Kitāb-] al-Khawwāṣṣ*, are also found. If this is so, [this stone] must indeed be truly special. This valley is abundant in thicket; there are reptiles in it, as we have noted in the description of vipers and similar [other animals] from among the big birds[53]. I know some people, who—when they want to pass the place where the rain-stones can be found, that is, the valley—[must choose from among] two roads. One of them is the place of the vipers, so it cannot be passed; the other is the place of the rain-stones. This is safe and not slippery, except at the place of the diamonds. Note that! I seem to recall meeting someone who decided to come out from the country of the Turks, descend to the valley, and go from the villages (*al-quryāt*) ascending to the country of the Turks, and he applied felt to the hoofs of the horses, mules, riding animals, donkeys and cattle in order not to hit that stone. For if they do make them knock together, [the caravans] have a hard time passing through that place, so heavy are the rains that can be expected on account of the [stones] rubbing against one another.[54]

---

[53] I. e. predatory birds.

[54] Translated by I. Zimonyi. Arabic text in Kraus 1942—43, ii, pp. 75—6, note 5. Yaltkaya (1943, p. 694) also gives a Turkish translation from Jābir's unedited *Kitāb al-Baḥth*: Yazın en sıcak ve en parlak gününde bu yağmur taşları içi su doldurulmuş olan bir kabın içine konularak birbirine sürülecek olursa yağmur yağmağa başlar ki, bu yağmur taşı *Karloklar*'ın topraklarındaki bir derede bulunur. Orada aynı zamanda elmas de vardır. Fakat müthiş yılanlar ve yırtıcı kuşlar burada her zaman bir tehlike teşkil ederler. Bu dereden geçen yolcular hayvanların ayaklarına keçeler sararlar. Böyle yapmıyacak olurlarla hayvanlarının taşlara çarpmasından hâsil olur.

Al-Bīrūnī in his treatise on mineralogy quotes the account of the rain-stone in the valley of the Karluks after al-Rāzī as follows:

> Al-Rāzī claims in his *Kitāb al-Khawwāṣṣ* that there is a pass in the land of the Turks between the Kharlukh and the Pechenek [*bajanāk*]. If an army, or a flock of small cattle pass through it, wool is tied around the hoofs of the animals to thus soften their steps, lest the stones [of this pass] knock together, raise a dark mist and produce heavy rains. They can bring forth rain by means of these stones whenever they wish: [the rain-maker] enters water, puts one of the stones of that pass into his mouth, waves his hands, and then it rains. Ibn Zakariyyā' [al-Rāzī] does not give this story; however, the existence of [the rain-stone] is not disputed. It is said in the *Kitāb al-Nukhab* that the rain-stones, [originating from] the desert behind the valley of the Kharlukh, are black mingled with some red. The news of similar things has spread even in different kingdoms whose inhabitants do not communicate with each other, and there is a land so wide between the Kharlukh—the Kharlukh of our days will be discussed below—and the Pechenek [*bajanākiyya*], so far are they are from each other as East is far from West.
>
> Once a Turk brought me some stones, supposing that I would rejoice at seeing these stones, receive them favourably, and not raise any objection to them. I said to him "Bring forth some rain now, out of its season, or any time I wish! If this happens at the appropriate time, I shall take [the stones] from you, and I give you more [money] than you expected!" So he did as I said; he dipped the stones into water, then he threw the water in which the stones had been soaked towards the skies, and all the while he murmured and cried out, but he could not bring forth

> any rain; the only water that rained down was what he had himself thrown towards the skies. It is all the more astonishing that the tale [of the rain-stone] has spread even among the upper classes, and has impressed them, to say nothing about the masses. [The witnesses of the ceremony] quarrelled about it without having any proof to back them up. Some who had been present began to defend it, and attributed [its failure] to the differences in the conditions of the place, arguing that these stones had their effect only in the land of the Turks.[55]

The Karluks lived in the Western Altai and the Tarbaghatai Mountains, nomadising in the upper reaches of the Irtish River. They were subjects of the Türks, but in 742—745 they were part of the Uighur—Basmil—Karluk coalition which finally overthrew the Eastern Türk Empire. Relations between the allies soon turned sour, and the Karluks moved westward. After 745, they came to Semirechye. In 751 in the battle of Talas, they were in alliance with the advancing Arabs, fighting against the Western Türks and the Chinese. In 766, the Western Türk—Türgesh tribes submitted to the Karluks, who established themselves in the lands of the former Western Türk Empire. Here they

---

[55] Translated by I. Zimonyi. Arabic text in Krenkow (ed.) 1936—7, pp. 218—9. Yaltkaya (1943, p. 694) also gives a sort of summary of al-Rāzī's account as quoted by Naṣīr al-Dīn al-Ṭūsī's unedited *Tansuqname-ye Ilkhānī*: *Tensukname*'sinde bu taşın muhtelif renklileri olduğunu bildiren ve bu taşın muayyen bir hayvanın karnından çıkarıldığı hakkında bir rivayet dahi bulunduğunu söyliyen Naṣīr al-Ṭūsī *Uygurlar* arasında bu işi yapmağa mahsus *Getharbi* (my italics A. M. — this is a garbling of *ǰadačï*) denilen muayyen kimseler olduğunu yazdıktan sonra bu de Abū al-Rayḥān yağmur yağdıracak kimsenin suya gireceğini va ağzına bu taşlardan birini alarak ellerini sallıyacağını yazdığı halde Naṣīr Ṭūsī taşın suda ıslatıldıktan sonra asılı olarak bırakılacağını yazmakta ve *Muhammet Ibnü Zekeriya*'dan bu suretle nakletmektedir.

mixed with the local Iranian, mostly Sogdian, population, and, establishing close contacts with the Arabs, came under the influence of Islam. A tenth-century Persian geography, the *Ḥudūd al-'Ālam*, locates them south of the Balkhash Lake in the western parts of the T'ien-shan, identifying Talas (Ṭarāz) as "a borough where both Muslims and Turks live. (This) locality is a residence of merchants, and the Gate of the Khallukh (*dar-i-Khallukh*)".[56] An important trade route crossed the Western T'ien-shan, starting from Shāsh through Isfijāb, Ṭarāz and Balasaghun, passing by Lake Issyk-Kul and leading to the Turfan Basin.[57]

The "valley of the Karluks" should be sought in this region, somewhere along the caravan routes passing by Lake Issyk-Kul. It can only be conjectured whether the custom of applying felt to the hoofs of riding and baggage-animals belongs to the domain of myths or that of reality. If the latter, its probable aim was to prevent

---

[56] Minorsky 1937, p. 119.

[57] For further details, see Minorsky 1937, pp. 286–97.

the animals from falling on the slippery rocks. Al-Rāzī's hint at the "land of the Turks between the Kharlukh and the Pecheneks" cannot be taken as a reference to a Karluk—Pecheneg border[58]: between the Karluks and the Pechenegs, there lived the Oghuz, and Bīrūnī himself, commenting on al-Rāzī, says that "there is a broad land between the Kharlukh and the Pechenek" in substantiation of his claim that the rain-stone of the Turks was widely known (see *Map 1*).

To return to the legend on the origin of the rain-stone from the mountains of the East, we can safely identify the mythical land of the rising sun with the mountains in the land of the Karluks, geographically speaking, with the western parts of the T'ien-shan. This identification, however, has further implications: the legend on the origin of the rain-stone from the mountains of the East relates how an ancestor of the Oghuz king's son, Balqīq al-Jabbūya, acquires the rain-stone from the land of the Karluks. In other words, the two legends are different versions of one and the same story on how the rain-stone came to be transferred from the Karluks to the Oghuz.

The mythical character of the legends notwithstanding, they refer to some real, historical events. It is significant that, though the ruler is not himself involved in weather-magic, the rain-stone appears in the sources as a sort of attribute of sovereignty that can be understood in terms of its use as a tactical device in warfare. In one of the ancestral legends of the Türks, it was A-shih-na's grandfather who had control over the weather. In the case of the Uighurs, Tamīm ibn Baḥr explicitly says that "[the rain-stones] are especially in the possession of the king of the Toquzoghuz and no other of their kings possesses them". This statement suggests that within a Turkic realm, the rain-stone, *i.e.* control over the weather, was an attribute of authority: only the ruling tribe possessed it. After the tribes of the Karluk confederation migrated to Semirechye (745), they were no longer subject to the Uighurs (766), and they, too, could

[58] Golden 1972, p. 58.

possess the rain-stone. Similarly, the Oghuz's acquisition of the rain-stone from the Karluks related in the two variants of the stone's legendary origin may be interpreted as a conflict between the Karluks and the Oghuz, more precisely, as a reference to the Oghuz managing to shake off Karluk hegemony.

This supposition is in keeping with the historical setting of the ninth century. The independent Karluk realm founded in 766 in the former On-oq—Türgesh lands in Semirechye was further strengthened after the fall of the Uighur Empire in Mongolia in 840, so that by the mid-ninth century, the Karluks had acquired hegemony over the peoples of the steppes.[59] The Karluk Empire, however, began to totter when, in 893, the Sāmānid amīr, Ismā'īl ibn Aḥmad, set out on a campaign against Talas, the royal residence of the Karluks. Its decline allowed the Oghuz and the Kimäks to establish empires of their own.[60]

Ismā'īl ibn Aḥmad's campaign against Talas has still another bearing on weather-magic. The story is, again, recounted by Yāqūt[61]:

> Abū al-'Abbās said: I have heard Ismā'īl ibn Aḥmad al-Sāmānī, the amīr of Khurāsān, saying: "There was a year when I attacked the Turks with an army of about twenty thousand Muslims. Sixty thousand of them armed to the teeth came against me. I fought against them for some days when one day, when I was in combat with them, some of the Turkic pages and others from among the Turks whose safety was guaranteed approached me and said: 'We have kinsmen and brothers in the army of the infidels, who warned us of the arrival of someone whom they mentioned as a soothsayer (*kāhin*) among them. According to their beliefs, he is able to produce clouds of hail, snow, etc., to

[59] Golden 1990, pp. 348—52.

[60] Zimonyi 1990, pp. 170—5.

[61] *Mu'jam al-Buldān*, ii, pp. 24—6.

attack anyone he wishes to destroy. Allegedly, he intends to procure a great hail-storm to fall on our army, so that every man that is hit by the hailstones will be killed.' I rebuked them and said: 'Infidelity has not yet been uprooted from your hearts. Is a human being able to do such a thing?' They said: 'We warned you, you will see for yourself tomorrow at dawn.' The following day, at dawn, a great cloud appeared over the foot of the mountain where my army was based, and it continued to spread and increase in size until it cast a shadow over the whole of my army. I was alarmed at the sight of its blackness and at hearing its frightful sounds. I realized that insubordination was inevitable, so I got off my horse and prostrated myself in prayer, while the members of my army surged about in turmoil as they had no doubt of impending disaster. I called upon God, pressing my face to the ground, and said: 'Oh, God, help us! Your servants are too feeble to do harm or to be beneficial. Oh, God, if this cloud brings rain upon us, the Muslims will rise in revolt, and the infidels will attack. Keep away the disaster from us by your power and strength!' I kept on praying for a long while with my face to the ground, being torn between greed and fear of God Most High; as you know, benefits come only from Him, and only He can avert disaster. I was still thus occupied, when pages and others from the army came to me bringing news that all was well, and they took my upper arm and set me on my feet from off my prayer carpet, and said: 'Look, oh, Amīr!' I raised my head, and saw that the cloud had moved away from my army and proceeded towards the army of the Turks, raining down big hail-stones upon them, and then they were surging, as their horses bolted and their tents were uprooted, and those of them that had been hit by hail-stones were either disabled, or killed. My companions recommended 'Let us attack them!' I said 'No, for God's punishment is subtler and more bitter.' Only a few of them escaped, and they fled leaving behind all that was in their camp. When the following day we reached the camp, we found an indescribable quantity of booty there, which we carried away. We extolled God for escaping from the danger, and we were aware that it was He who had facilitated this for us. We took possession of the booty."

These are the stories I wrote down as I found them: only God knows if they are true.[62]

Since the narrative, supposedly told by Ismā'īl ibn Aḥmad himself, describes a campaign on a grand scale led personally by the Sāmānid ruler against the Turks, it can be surmised that this was the campaign which Ismā'īl ibn Aḥmad waged against the Karluks in 893. It led to the fall of Talas, the Karluk ruler's residence. The Sāmānid army sacked the town and got away with an immense booty.[63]

Ismā'īl ibn Aḥmad's story of the Turkic heathen weather-magician is not the only evidence that weather-magic was known in Sāmānid Iran which the Turks used in war. We find a surprisingly similar event related in Firdausī's *Shāhnāma*. The battle in which magic was used against the Iranian army is recounted in the chapter on Kai Khusrau, but it can be assumed to reflect some much later historical events, namely, the wars between the Sāmānids and the Turks which took place approximately a century before Firdausī's time:

---

[62] Translated by I. Zimonyi.

[63] This event is described by several Islamic authors, who speak of the Karluks (Mas'ūdī) or of the Turks (Ṭabarī) as the enemies of the Sāmānid ruler; see Zimonyi 1990, pp. 170–2.

Amongst the Turks [*turkān*] there was a man named Bāzur, who had travelled everywhere in the practice of enchantment [*afsūn*], having learned the arts of chicanery [*kažžī*] and magic [*jādu 'ī*] and acquired a knowledge of Chinese and Pahlavi. To this wizard Pirān[64] said,

'Go from here to the highest mountain summit and suddenly on to the Iranians cause a storm of snow, frost and raging wind to descend.'

As soon as the wizard had reached his destination, there came a storm of snow and furious wind, which so disabled the hands of the Iranian spearsmen that they could not engage in combat. In that moment of terror and intense cold the cry of the Turānian warriors was heard, accompanied by a rain of arrows. At the same time Pirān was commanding his troops on the field of battle to launch an immediate assault, and, since the Iranians' hands were frozen on to their spears, none was able to show fight. Humān[65] then uttered a shout and rushed like a demon into attack, and so many Iranians were thus slain that a river of blood flowed in the midst of them. Both valley and plain were covered with snow and blood and the Iranian horsemen were thrown into headlong confusion. Commander and captains raised woeful petitions to Heaven, saying,

'Thou who art too lofty for men's knowledge, mind or comprehension, who art above no place or within any place and yet dost exist in every place, we all are Thy sinful slaves and in our helplessness call to Thee for justice. Thou art an aid in man's sore straits and hast

---

[64] Commander of the Turanians, that is, of the Turks.

[65] A Turanian hero, Pirān's brother.

power over fire and frost; deliver us from this intensity of cold, for apart from Thee we recognize no lord.'

There arrived at that moment a man who was a student of the sciences and pointed out to Rahhām[66] the place on the mountain where the vile Bāzur stood exercising his enchantments and wizardry. Thereupon Rahhām turned away from the scene of battle and rode his horse out of the midst of the troops. Midway up the slope he left the road and climbed on foot to the summit. There the wizard caught sight of him and advanced to attack him, holding in his hand a pole of Chinese steel. But as he approached, Rahhām swiftly plucked a sword from his belt and with its sharp blade cut off the other's hand. Suddenly a wind arose as though it were the Day of Resurrection and in front of the storm the black cloud was carried away. Down from the mountain now descended the warrior Rahhām, first having imprisoned the wizard's remaining arm, and coming on to the plain, he remounted his horse. The weather now had returned to what it had been before, the sun shone and the skies were blue.[67]

Structurally, Yāqūt's account of Ismā'īl ibn Aḥmad and the passage cited above from the *Shāhnāma* are, beyond a doubt, the same. The weather-magician of the Turkic army sends a storm over the Sāmānid troops, and the Iranians, with the help of their own God, drive it away. The *Shāhnāma* contains an additional element: besides entreating God, the storm can be averted also by killing the weather-magician. Firdausī gives a truly realistic description of how the Iranian warriors were disabled by

---

[66] An Iranian hero, one of the twelve champions.

[67] The *Shāhnāma* is quoted in Levy's (1967, pp. 130–1) prose translation, the Persian text is in Vullers 1878–84, ii, pp. 891–5.

the tempest. It is noteworthy that weather-magic appears in these sources roughly in the same geographical setting and in the same historical milieu as in the cases discussed above, namely in connection with the Karluks in the Western T'ien-shan at the end of the ninth century.

The second source that can be connected to the Karluks with a high degree of probability is a Sogdian text, the *P 3*[68] discovered by Stein in the "Caves of the Thousand Buddhas", which provides a detailed description of weather-magic. Though the text has an Indian background, it does not seem to be a translation, and was labelled a "shamanist rain-makers's handbook" by Henning.[69] This text deserves special attention as the only detailed specific description of weather-magic known to date from the eighth and ninth centuries. The first part of the text contains an enumeration and description of different stones that have some medicinal, protective or harmful effects[70], and then there follows the description of weather-magic proper[71]:

> Si l'homme veut faire le charme, il doit faire l'«édifice magique» à 25 têtes (?) [125] et l'étendre sur une grande rive; soit auprès du grand étang, soit auprès de l'eau courante, soit au bord d'une source il doit étendre l' «édifice magie» et sur un rideau (?) bleu, dessiner l'eau du mahāsamudra, [130] les nāgas dans l'eau, le gandharva aquatique, et le grand..... plein d'eau. Sur le dos il dessinera, jusqu'à la frange (?), des nāgas variés: l'un

---

[68] Catalogued as Ch. 0093.b. Fr.; its facsimile edited by Stein (1921, Vol. iv, Plate CLVIII); the text edited and translated by Reichelt (1931, pp. 61—5), re-edited and commented by Benveniste (1940, pp. 59—73), and commented by Henning (1945, p. 465, note 2, 1946, pp. 726—30) and Sims-Williams (1976, p. 46).

[69] 1946, p. 714.

[70] Lines 1—122.

[71] Lines 123—304.

[135] avec une tête de serpent, un autre avec une tête de cheval, un autre avec une tête d'éléphant, un autre avec une tête de lion, un autre avec une tête de tigre, un autre avec une tête de panthère, un autre avec une tête de porc, un autre avec une tête de chien, un autre avec une tête de boeuf, un autre avec une tête d'âne, un autre avec une tête d'oiseau, [140] un autre avec une tête d'homme, un autre avec une tête de dieu, un autre avec une tête de poisson, un autre avec une tête de yaksa (?), un autre avec une tête de divers fauves, un autre avec des têtes variées. Il étendra cet «édifice magique» de l'intérieur de l'eau du côté du levant. [145] Puis de nouveau sur un autre rideau (?) bleu de ciel, il dessinera la lune brillante. Il faut (y) dessiner les 12 étoiles dans leur demeure sur le mont Sumeru, et les 28 étoiles et [150] les 10 grands diables effrayants et le reste des constellations (et) des astres, il faut tous les dessiner.

Il dessinera en outre, avec leurs diverses apparences et formes, l'ensemble des nuages, tous [155] sous l'aspect de nāgas, chacun avec son corps et sa tête, et étendra cette tenture à l'intérieur de l' «édifice magique», du côté du levant, en manière de ciel. Puis la précédente tenture, il l'étendra dans l' «édifice magique» [160] sur le sol propre. Dans l' «édifice magique», il balaiera d'abord bien soigneusement et fera un mandala à quatre coins; il faudra les pierres des neuf sortes qui ont été décrites plus haut. Il remplira [165] le chaudron plein d'eau et pressera ces pierres des neuf sortes, et les jettera toutes dans l'eau. Il y jettera à la fois les pierres et l'eau.........[170] Cela s'appelle........ et .... Qu'il prenne du camphre, du santal, de l'onguent, du ......, du costus, du ....., du sel ammoniac en morceaux, du safran, de l'aloès, et fasse une drogue de tout cela [175] et la coupe très fin et la jette avec ces pierres dans le chaudron. Il allumera du feu par dessous (?) de manière que peu à peu la fumée monte. Il doit faire du... [180] de santal blanc et de même que sur le dessin (?)....., il y a un....., de même il y faut graver (?) le ..... de telle mainère que le chameau se batte (?) avec le chameau, le cheval avec [185] le cheval, l'âne avec l'âne, le boeuf avec le boeuf, le mouton avec le mouton, le chien avec le chien, l'oiseau avec l'oiseau, [190] l'homme avec l'homme. Cette gravure (?), il la fera graver (?) entièrement sur le....., par un bon artisan. Il le mettra sur pied là où se trouve l'eau de chaudron. Puis [195] de cette drogue il appliquera un peu sur le ... de santal. Et il ordonnera à l'artiste de bien dessiner sur ... le petit vent de sept sortes, et par-dessous de dessiner à l'aiguille la braise (?) [200] et suspendre le .... à la braise (?). Quand il aura achevé ce travail, après avoir fini, il doit s'agenouiller et dire: «Je te rends hommage, Vent parfumé (et) juste (?), Vent victorieux (et) puissant, [205] à la décision rapide, accorde-moi ainsi une faveur, Vent vaillant! Parfumé, orné de rouge, fils du Dieu Suprême, ô Toi! sois-moi pitoyable, et dans l'intérêt de tous les êtres des sept espèces, [210] accorde-moi maintenant une faveur pour le pays. Donne-moi à présent une force telle que le nuage se lève et que la pluie bienfaisante tombe, pour que la culture réussisse et que les pousses [215] et les plantes médicinales croissent, que la communauté entière ait une pure pourriture, soit satisfaite, fortifiée et apaisée, à cause de ta gloire et de ta force.

Là-dessus, il faut faire grand [220] serment aux nāgas avec le mahākāla et ce dispositif (?) dont je viens de parler. Puis lorsque tout sera complètement fait, il faut que les nāgas avec le vent viennent à [225] l'endroit même où l'on veut produire pluie et rosée. Quand le vent mugira, il faut enflammer les grenouilles et le .... et les mettre sur la porte de l' «édifice», envelopper les grenouilles avec un feutre noir et les mettre [230] sous l'eau. Quand il commencera à pleuvoir un peu, le sorcier doit monter sur un cheval bai, prendre la bride dans ses mains, l'agiter sept fois du côté du levant [235] et sept fois de côté du couchant, appeler fortemet trois fois à haute voix avec force et vigueur, Il doit suspendre sous la bride des plumes de vautour et de faisan. Puis il [240] pressera l'onguent. Le sorcier appliquera l'onguent sur son visage. Quand il commencera à pleuvoir, s'il ne pleut pas réellement fort, alors il revêtira une peau de loup et tournera [245] sept fois de suite autour de l' «édifice» en poussant de grands hurlements avec la voix du loup. S'il ne pleut pas réellement fort, alors il prendra un serpent et le suspendra à l'envers également (?), il attachera le chat sauvage d'un même côté. [250] Puis il attachera la grenouille auprès de l'eau. Il attachera l'animal à un angle; il attachera la peau de loup à un angle; il attachera l'oiseau à un angle; il attachera le chien [255] à un angle, de manière que tous ces êtres aient peur le premier du second et l'un de l'autre. Alors en conséquence, il se produit une grande pluie.

Mais si éventuellement [260] il commence au contraire à faire froid, il faut cette fois enlever les ..... du vent, enlever les pierres de l'eau, les mettre au dehors et faire un feu brûlant. Après cela, il ne fera plus froid.

Lorsque la pluie semblera ainsi [265] suffisante et qu'on désire qu'il ne pleuve plus, il faut enlever les nuages des ..... et les pierres et les réunir (?) et aussitôt la pluie cessera.

Si l'on désire qu'il fasse beau, on doit employer [270] du camphre, du souchet blanc, du santal blanc, du safran et de l'onguent et faire de tout cela un baume, le couper très fin. Il faut un os do mouton. On y fera un trou

> et en tirera la moelle. [275] On mélangera le baume avec la moelle de mouton tout ensemble et on l'appliquera sur la maison.
>
> S'il désire maintenant que le jour soit clair, il s'enduira le visage et les yeux de ce baume, [280] et aussitôt il fera clair. Mais s'il ne fait pas clair après cela, il faut en outre une tête d'animal noir. Il ne la brisera pas, mais la fera cuire intacte et la tirera (?) en bon état de la cuisson [285]. Il y fera un trou au front. Il apportera du mastic, de la mauve musquée, de la coloquinte et du ... et les coupera très fin ensemble, pour que (cela) soit très fin, les mélangera avec la moelle de mouton et en fera huit [290] boules. Ces boules, il les mettra dans la tête d'animal; il mettra deux boules aux yeux, il mettra deux boules au nez; il mettra deux boules aux oreilles; il mettra [295] deux boules dans la bouche. Il dressera un lomg (morceau de) bois auprès de la fenêtre de l' «édifice» et (y) mettra cette tête du côté de la fenêtre. Après cela, il fera aussitôt clair.
>
> [300] Si la pluie ne cessa pas, mais s'il continue à pleuvoir, il lavera vite le chaudron et versera cette eau sur le sol. Puis il placera un miroir du côté du soleil. Et la pluie cessera aussitôt.[72]

At first glance, it would seem to be rather difficult to show that the rites described in this Sogdian text—which contains no hint of ethnic names—have any bearing on the Karluks, or even on the Turks. Indeed, the text is of a syncretic character, containing Indian, Iranian and some other Inner Asian elements, as already noticed by Henning.[73] Only the

[72] Ed. and transl. by Benveniste 1940, pp. 65—73; the Sogdian text runs in parallel columns on the same page.

[73] 1946, p. 714.

later Turkic parallels with certain rites mentioned in the text (weather-magic done by means of a dark-coloured horse), and the linguistic analysis of *cδy-kr'y mrty*, the name of the weather-magician in *P 3*, will reveal that this Sogdian text may well be connected with the Karluks.

THE KARAKHANIDS

What we know of Turkic weather-magic from the above-mentioned chronicles is, to our good fortune, supplemented by that most comprehensive and authoritative of sources on the eleventh-century customs and beliefs of the Turks of Central Asia—and the Karakhānid Turks in particular—Maḥmūd al-Kāshgharī's *Dīwān Lughāt al-Turk*.[74] Kāshgharī is the first to mention that in Turkic weather-magic, *i.e.* "divination (*kahāna*) with stones to bring on rain and wind," is called *yāt* in Turkic.[75] Elsewhere he writes:

> *Yat* is a type of divination (*kahāna*) using special stones with which one brings on rain, wind, etc. It is well known among them.[76] I myself witnessed it in Yaghma where it was performed to put out a fire that had broken out. Snow fell in the summer, by the leave of God Most High, and put out the fire in my presence.[77]

The Turkic weather-magician of whom Yāqūt and Firdausī speak is easy to recognize in the figure of the *yātčï* whose activities are described by Kāshgharī in accounts like the following:

---

[74] On the Turkic customs, beliefs and superstitions in Kāshgharī's *Dīwān*, see Brockelmann 1925 and Dankoff 1975.

[75] Dankoff—Kelly 1982—85, ii, p. 230.

[76] *I.e.* the Turks.

[77] *Op.cit.*

> *Yat* is a type of divination (*kahāna*) using special stones with which one brings on rain, wind, etc. It is well known among them.[76] I myself witnessed it in Yaghma where it was performed to put out a fire that had broken out. Snow fell in the summer, by the leave of God Most High, and put out the fire in my presence.[77]

The Turkic weather-magician of whom Yāqūt and Firdausī speak is easy to recognize in the figure of the *yātčï* whose activities are described by Kāshgharī in accounts like the following:

> *Yātčï yatladï* The diviner (*kāhin*) performed a divination (*takahhana*) with stones for clouds and rain.[78] *beg yatlattï* The amir ordered the diviner to bring forth wind and rain by divination (*amara l-kāhin ḥattā yatakahhana wa-jā la bi-r-rīḥ wa-l-amṭār*). This is well known in the country of the Turks; wind, hail and rain are brought forth with stones—by the leave of God Most High.[79]

Dankoff[80] is probably right that *ürüŋ* 'diviner's fee (*ḥulwān al-kāhin*)' applies to the *yātčï* as well, though *yātčï*s are not mentioned *expressis verbis* in connection with diviner's fees.[81]

The *Ta'rīkh-i Fakhru 'd-Dīn Mubārakshāh*, completed in 1206, which mentions rain-stones in connection with the Turks in general, was written nearest to the Karakhanids both geographically and chronologically, so it might be informative to quote it here:

---

[76] *I.e.* the Turks.

[77] *Op.cit.*

[78] *Op.cit.*, p. 307.

[79] *Op.cit.*, p. 141.

[80] 1975, p. 77.

[81] *ürüŋ* literally means 'white' (Clauson 1972, p. 233). Besides the *yātčï*, the *qām* 'shaman' also termed *al-kāhin* by Kāshghārī (Dankoff 1975, p. 76).

There occur two stones in Turkistān which, if placed one on the other crosswise and stained with the blood of a maiden and set on a pole in the desert, and a fistful of earth is thrown at them, whereupon the whole earth becomes dark and the ground begins to ooze water. Until the stones are removed, washed and concealed at a place, the darkness and the oozing of the earth will not diminish, and there will be no light on earth.

There are two other stones, which are placed crosswise one on the other and set on a pole in the desert and stained with the blood of a woman who has recently brought forth and the stone is sprinkled with a fistful of water, dew begins to fall, and it frightfully thunders. If a ladle is thrown into the fire in the meanwhile, terrifying a thunderbolt appears, and it is lightning. Until the stones are removed and washed, the lightning does not cease. Most of their magicians possess such stones as these.[82]

THE KHWĀRAZMSHĀHS

The power of the Karakhanid Empire was destroyed by the Khwārazmshāhs, at whose imperial court weather-magic played a particularly important role. In spite of being ardent followers of Islam, the Khwārazmshāhs fostered some heathen Turkic practices. Detailed accounts of rain-making rituals have come down to us from the reigns of the last two Khwārazmshāhs, ʿAlāʾ al-Dīn Muḥammad (1200—1220), and his son, Jalāl al-Dīn (1220—1231). How and where rain-stones were to be found, and how they were employed at ʿAlāʾ al-Dīn Muḥammad's court are narrated by Abū l-ʿAbbās Aḥmad ibn Yūsuf ibn Aḥmad al-Tīfāshī[83] (d.

[82] Ross 1927, p. x, Persian text pp. 41–2.
[83] Ullmann 1972, pp. 125–6.

1253) in his *Kitāb Azhār al-Afkār fī Jawāhir al-Aḥjar* "The Flower of What Is Known of Precious Stones":

> Rien de plus commun, dit-il, et plus authentique, chez les peuples de l'Orient, que l'existence de certaines pierres par le moyen desquelles on fait tomber la pluie. Un homme d'une véracité scrupuleuse m'a assuré que se trouvant en Perse, entre Bokhara et Samarkand, dans l'armée du sultan Ala-eldin-Mohammed, souverain du Khawarizm, il vit un Turc qui savait faire usage des pierres dont nous allons parler, et qui faisait descendre une pluie abondante, toutes les fois qu'il plaisait au prince. Il ajouta que, dans les contrées de la Chine et la Perse, on trouve un oiseau qui porte le nom de *sorkhāb*[84], c'est-à-dire *rouge aquatique*, parce que, dans la langue du pays, *sorkh* signifie *rouge* et *áb* signifie *l'eau*. Cet oiseau est de la taille d'une grosse oie et les plumes rouges. C'est le même qui, en Égypte, porte le nom de *baschmour*, et que les tireurs d'arquebuse connaissent sous celui de *mirzam*. Il est commun dans ce pays, et l'on emploie ses plumes pour les suspendre aux chars en guise d'ornement. Dans la Chine et les provinces de Perse qui confinent à cette contrée, l'oiseau dont nous parlons fait son nid dans des îles écartées, à l'époque des pluies et des torrents. Lorsque les eaux se retirent, on va à recherche de ces nids, et l'on creuse en dessous la profondeur de deux coudées. On y trouve une pierre grosse comme un oeuf, de couleur cendrée, avec des points blancs et rouges. Elle est très-friable, et celle qui a cette qualité au plus haut point est réputée la meilleure. On recueille avec soin toutes les pierres de ce genre que l'on peut découvrir,

---

[84] *surkhāb* 'a sort of water-fowl; also called *kharchāl* (anas casarca)' (Steingass 1892, p. 672): the ruddy goose (*Casarca ferruginea* or *Casarca ferruginea*).

et on les porte au trésor du souverain. On les dépose dans un coffre, confié à la garde d'un intendant, chargé spécialement de ce soin, et qui seul en a la clef. Pendant l'été, lorsque le prince, dans quelque marche, se trouve incommodité de la chaleur ou de la poussière, qu'il veut ou se délivrer d'un siége, ou empêcher les invasions d'un ennemi, ou sauver son armée, ou qu'enfin quelque circonstance exige une pluie abondante et une atmosphère humide, l'intendant chargé du soin de ces pierres reçoit l'ordre d'en faire incessamment usage. Un habitant de Gaznah, qui assista à cette opération dans l'armée du sultan susdit, m'a donné là-dessus les détails qu'on va lire: Je vis, dit-il, arriver un vieillard, turc de nation. On lui dressa une tente qui le dérobait à la vue du reste de l'armée, mais dans laquelle j'entrai avec l'intendant chargé de la garde des pierres. Le haut de la tente, du côté qui regarde le ciel, était entièrement découvert. On plaça devant cet homme un vase rempli d'eau. Il prit trois roseaux assez gros, il en dressa l'un à droite et l'autre à la gauche du vase; pour le troisième, il l'étendit en travers, et en lia les deux bouts à l'extrémité supérieure des deux premiers roseaux. Ensuite il tira un serpent dont le corps était mince, et dont la couleur, comme celle des pierres, était grise et marquée de taches rouges et blanches. Il lui lia la queue avec un fil, et le suspendit au roseau qui formait la traverse, en sorte que l'animal était dans une position renversée, ayant la tête à environ deux coudées au-dessus de l'eau. Le Turc ayant reçu des mains de l'intendant deux de ces pierres dont nous avons parlé, les mit dans l'eau, puis les retira, les frotta légèrement l'une contre l'autre et les rejeta dans le vase. Il répéta la même chose sept fois de suite, aprés quoi il prit l'eau, dont il fit une aspersion à terre. Pendant l'opération il avait la tête nue (ainsi qu'il est expressément ordonné), les cheveux épars, et le visage refrogné comme celui d'un

> homme en colère. Il élevait sa tête vers le ciel, en prononçant certaines paroles par lesquelles il semblait appeler la pluie. Tout cela durait l'espace de deux heures; et bientôt après le ciel se couvrait de nuages, et la pluie tombait en abondance.
>
> Celui de qui je tiens ces détails m'a assuré qu'il avait assité plusieurs fois à cette expérience, et que le succès en avait toujours été le même. Nous étions, me dit-il, au coeur de l'été, et le ciel était absolument sans nuage. Cependant, lorsque je retournais à ma tente, je trouvais tout le chemin coupé par bourbiers et des torrents. Le vieillard turc, ajoutait-il, m'a raconté que toutes les fois qu'il mettait ce secret en pratique, il éprouvait infailliblement quelque malheur, la mort d'un enfant, d'un parent, ou la perte d'une partie de son bien, ou quelque autre accident semblable; qu'il restait toujours pauvre, et ne recevait de sultan que l'équivalent de ce qu'il avait perdu. Ce secret n'est pratique que par un certain nombre de personnes qui en ont exclusivement la connaisance.[85]

Tīfāshī goes on to tell about ꜥAlāʾ al-Dīn Muḥammad's campaign against the Karakhanids, which took place in 1212:

> Le même homme de qui je tiens ces faits, et plusieurs Persans aussi instruits que véridiques, m'ont assuré à plusieurs reprises que le sultan du Khawarizm[86], le même dont nous avons déjà parlè, voulut porter la guerre dans la partie du pays des Turcs qui touche à la Chine. Lorsqu'il était près d'y entrer, il éprouva sans interruption des pluies, du froid et une neige excessives, en sorte que toute son armée fut sur le point de périr; cependant ce prince, qui

---

[85] Quatremère 1836, pp. 432–3.
[86] *I.e.* ꜥAlāʾ al-Dīn Muḥammad.

> connaissait la température froide de ces contrées, avait eu le soin de choisir, pour son expédition, la saison de l'été, où il ne devait pas avoir à redouter de pareils accidents. Se doutant bien que cette variation de l'atmosphère n'était pas naturelle, il envoya ses gardes avec ordre de parcourir toutes les montagnes du pays. Ils lui amenèrent deux hommes qu'ils avaient surpris au moment où ils mettaient en oeuvre les pierres dont il a été question. Le sultan les fit envelopper dans deux couvertures de feutre noires et enterrer tout vivants, car c'est le moyen infaillible d'arrêter sur-le-champs la neige, la pluie et le froid; sinon l'effet du sortilège se prolonge un temps considérable. Si deux personnes pratiquent ce secret dans deux endroits à la fois, la neige et le froid deviennent si excessifs, que l'on ne peut les supporter.[87]

It is interesting to note, that a few years later, during the winter of 1217—18, snowstorms of unusual severity stopped ʿAlāʾ al-Dīn Muḥammad's forces in another campaign in Kurdistān and Luristān.[88]

ʿAlāʾ al-Dīn Muḥammad's son, Jalāl al-Dīn, the last of the Khwārazmshāhs, had weather-magic performed in 1229 at Velāsjird, near the fortress town of Akhlat on the northwest shore of Lake Van. The event is recounted by the Sultan's secretary and biographer, Shihāb al-Dīn Muḥammad ibn Aḥmad ʿAlī al-Nasawī, in his work written in 1261:

> Au moment où l'on arriva à Velachguerd, les populations se plaignaient de la violence de la chaleur, du manque de pluies et aussi du tourment que font souffrir les mouches aux hommes et aux animaux. On résolut alors de provoquer la chute de la pluie à l'aide de ces pierres (dont il a été question plus haut). A la vérite, nous étions tout d'abord

[87] Quatremère *op. cit.*, pp. 433–4.
[88] Bosworth 1978, p. 1068.

> parfaitement incrédules à l'endroit de leur efficacité, mais nous dùmes constater plus tard, à plusieurs reprises, qu'elles avaient une influence réelle sur le destin. Peut-être cependant, en cette circonstance, avons-nous été dupes d'une illusion ou d'une erreur, comme tant d'autres l'ont été avant nous.
>
> Le sultan dirigea en personne le cérémonie pendant son séjour dans la plaine de Velachguerd et la pluie ne cessa de tomber, à plusieurs reprises, nuit et jour, si bien que les gens, contrariés et ennuyés de sa persistance, se prirent à regretter l'operation magique qui avaient été faite. Il y avait une boue et des fondrières telles qu'il était presque impossible de parvenir jusqu'à la tente du sultan. J'ai entendu, à ce sujet, la nourrice de la khatoun assurer qu'elle avait dit au sultan: «Tu es une sorte de *Bâkhudavend ʿalem* (c'est-à-dire Maître de l'univers. Et, les gens qui l'abordaient ne lui donnaient pas l'autre titre). Mais ce n'est pas dans l'art de faire tomber la pluie, car tu as causé bien du tort à tout le monde en produisant un pareil déluge; un autre qui toi n'aurait pas agi ainsi, il n'aurait fait tomber que juste la quantité d'eau nécessaire.» — «Les choses ne sont pas du tout ce que tu crois, répondit-il; cette pluie est un indice de mon pouvoir et mon pouvoir ne saurait étre comparè à celui d'aucune des personnes de mon entourage.»[89]

The same story is narrated by Bailak ibn Muḥammad al-Qibchāqī in his work *Kanz al-Tijār fī Maʿrifat al-Aḥjār* "A Merchants' Treasury of Knowledge on Stones"[90]. This latter account, however, continues as follows:

---

[89] Houdas 1891–5, ii, pp. 396–7, Arabic text 1891, pp. 237–8.

[90] Ullmann 1972, p. 128.

Le samedi 10e jour du mois de moharram de l'an 674 j'étais assis à la porte de Dara, fils de Derbas, en dedans de la porte Saadah, au Caire, lorsqu'un jeune homme vint se placer à mon côté commença à s'entretenir avec moi. Lui ayant demandé quel était son nom, il me répondit qu'il s'appelait Azdemur, et qu'il était attaché à l'émir Tadj-eldin-Ali-bek de Khawarizm. Je lui dis alors: J'ai entendu raconter, au sujet de cet émir, qu'il avait de petites pierres au moyen desquelles il excitait le vent et faisait tomber la pluie. Il me répondit: Le fait est parfaitement vrai; cet émir possédait trois pierres, dont l'une était d'une forme allongée comme la tête d'une hache, et sa couleur tirait sur le gris; les deux autres étaient blanches et rondes. Il me confia la première avec l'étui dans lequel elle était renfermée: mais faute d'attention de ma part, elle ne tarda pas à se perdre. Voyant qu'il me la demandait, et craignant d'être battu en punition de ma négligence, je niai hardiment avoir reçu de lui aucun dépôt l'émir désespérant de recouvrer sa pierre, s'adressa à un autre personnage du Khawarizm qu'il savait posséder de semblables pierres, et qui lui en donna effectivement une. Nous étions alors dans la ville de Gazah sur la côte de la mer. Lorsque nous fûmes arrivés en Égypte, le sultan d'alors Moïzz-Aibek le Turcoman questionna l'émir au sujet des pierres susdites de leur vertu. Tadj-eldin attesta la vérité du fait, et en fit l'expérience à plusieurs reprises, en présence du sultan, dans le bourg nommé Barideh qui fait partie du canton d'Abbaseh. Chaque fois il produisit à son gré du vent et de la pluie. Pour cet effet il prenait une de ces pierres, la posait sur un morceau d'étoffe de coton, et égorgeait au-dessus un rat ou un serpent; en même temps il récitait en langue du Khawarizm des mots que nous ne comprenions pas.[91]

---

[91] Quatremère, *op. cit.*, p. 434.

This performance of weather-magic at Jalāl al-Dīn's command took place only a few years before his final defeat by the Mongols. The Mongol conquest brought about a dramatic change in the history of the Turkic peoples, and, as we shall see, in the history of weather-magic as well.

THE MONGOLS

The earliest pieces of evidence on weather-magic among the Mongol peoples date from the time of the Kitan Liao Dynasty (907—1125). Weather-magic, rain-making, to be precise, formed part of the official ceremonies at the imperial Liao court. As one of the rites that was of Kitan, rather than of Chinese, origin[92], it showed a remarkable resistance to the changes that were otherwise characteristic of Liao ceremonies.[93] Rain-magic performed at times of drought is described for the year 962: the Kitan emperor ordered his attendants to pour water on each other. Records for the year 1080 tell of the emperor praying for rain, after having ordered his left and right attendants to pour water on one another. In both cases, the ceremony was a success: the rains started to come down not much thereafter.[94]

The *Sê-sê* rain-ceremony was a rite of quite another kind:

> In case of drought an auspicious day was chosen for performing the Sê-sê Ceremony to pray for rain. Previous to this date an awning was set up with a hundred poles. When the day arrived, the emperor offered wine to the images of former emperors and then shot at willow trees. The emperor shot twice; the imperial princes and the ministers, in the order of their rank, each shot once. Those who hit the willow trees received as pledges the hats and

---

[92] Wittfogel—Fêng 1949, p. 18 and Franke 1990, p. 406.
[93] *Op. cit.*, p. 217 and 380.
[94] *Op. cit.*, p. 257 and 265.

robes of those who had marked the trees. Those who did not make a hit gave up their hats and robes as pledges. The losers offered wine to the winners. Afterwards the hats and coats were returned to each person.

Further, on the next day willow trees were planted southeast of the awning. The shamans making the sacrifices of wine and glutinous and panicled millet and praying, planted the willow trees. After the emperor and the empress had worshipped the east, the younger men shot at the willow trees. Members of the imperial clan and of the Imperial Maternal Uncles and the various courtiers who participated in the ceremony were granted presents accordingly to their rank. After three days, if rain fell, four horses and four suits of clothes were granted to the *ti-lieh-ma-tu*; if not, water was spilled upon him.[95]

This description dates from 1100, though the *Sê-sê* rain ceremony dated from long before this time. One source[96] indicates that it was established by Su Kaghan before the founding of the Liao Dynasty, probably still in T'ang times (618—906). The rite was distinguished by the emperor's participation in the ceremonies performed by religious functionaries who are called *ti-lieh-ma-tu* who was in charge of ritual and etiquette at the Liao court, and who also offered the sacrifices to the Mu-yeh Mountain[97]. In the case of the Kitans, therefore, there is no indication of the existence of specialized weather-magicians.

Entirely different was the weather-magic of the Mongols proper. There are several references to its use in warfare in the sources relating the history of Chinggis Khan and his successors. The earliest mention is of the Naimans using weather-magic against Chinggis Khan in the battle of Köiten in 1202, as recounted in the *Secret History of the Mongols*:

---

[95] *Op. cit.*, p. 267.

[96] *Op. cit.*, p. 267, note 136.

[97] *Op. cit.*, p. 217.

> Next day the troops were sent forward and when they met, at Köyiten, they engaged in combat. As they pressed each other downhill and uphill, and organized their forces, those very same Buyiruq-qan and Quduqa, knowing how to produce a rainstorm by magic, conjured up a storm. But the magic storm turned back and it was precisely upon them that the storm fell. They themselves could no longer advance and tumbled into ravines. They said: "We are not loved by Heaven!", and dispersed.[98]

Another case of its use is recorded for 1232 in connection with Tolui's campaign against the Jürchen, as described in Juvaini's *Ta'rīkh-i Jahāngushā*:

> Among the Mongols was a Qanqli who was well versed in the science of *yai*, that is the use of the rain-stone. Ulugh-Noyan commanded him to begin practicing his art and ordered the whole army to put on raincoats over their winter clothes and not to dismount from their horses for three days and nights. The Qanqli busied himself with his *yai* so that it began to rain behind the Mongols, and on the last day the rain was changed to snow, to which was added a cold wind. From this excessive summer chill, which was such as they had not experienced in winter, the Khitayan army were disheartened and dismayed and the Mongol army emboldened and exhilarated. Finally—
>
> When the red jewel of morning distinguished the

---

[98] Rachewiltz 1974, pp. 65–6. Mongolian text: *143 manaqarsi yabu'ulju gürülcejü köyiten bayi[l]duju doroqsi de'eksi iquriqaldun jibsi'erülcen büküi-tür müt buyiruq- qan quduqa qoyar jada medekün aju'ui jadalaqun bolun jada hurbaju müt anu de'ere jada bolju'u müt yabun yadaju nuras-tur quladu'at tenggeri-de ese ta'alaqdaba bida ke'eldü'et butaraju'ui* (Rachewiltz 1972, p. 62).

white from the black

> —they beheld the army of Khitai like a flock of sheep— 'the head of one at the tail of another'—huddled together in groups on account of the coldness of the weather and the excessive chill, their heads and feet tucked in like hedgehogs and their weapons frozen with ice—'*and thou mightiest have seen the people laid low, as though they had been the trunks of hollow palms*.'[99] The *yaichi* now ceased his *yai*, and the army issued forth behind them and like hawks falling upon a flock of pigeons, nay like lions charging upon a herd of deer, they turned upon those deer-necked ones with the eyes of wild cows, the gait of partridges and the appearance of peacocks and attacked them from every side.[100]

It is clear from the context that what Juvaini[101] is describing here is Kangli and not Mongolian weather-magic. The Kanglis appear in the sources as a tribe of the Kipchaks, or in connection with the Kimäks who lived in southwestern Siberia, their territory extending as as far as the Syr Darya and to the fringes of Turkestan. The thirteenth-century sources speak of the Kanglis as neighbours of the Naimans. They, too, were defeated by the Mongols, and those who survived served in the Mongolian army. It was possibly a Kangli soldier conscripted into Tolui's army in this way who was ordered to perform the weather-magic. The ritual is not described, but both Juvaini and Vaṣṣāf insert explanatory notes into their narratives (*ʿilm-i yāy, yaʿnī istiʿmāl-i ḥajar al-maṭar*) to the effect that the 'art of weather-magic *yāy*' means the 'use of the rain-stone'. It is also worth noting that the term for 'weather-magic' is not Mongolian (which would be *ǰada*). The words *yāy* and *yāyčï* may well have been the terms used by the

[99] Koran 69:7.

[100] Boyle 1958, i, p. 193; Persian text Qazvīnī 1912, pp. 152–3.

[101] The story is also narrated by Vaṣṣāf (Hammer–Purgstall 1856, p. 146).

Kanglis themselves, and Bosworth[102] rightly remarks that the discussed passage in Juvaini is our only clue to the religion specific to the Kanglis.

Rashīd al-Dīn relates the same event, and his account reveals more about the circumstances of the use of *jadamīshī*:

> Tolui Khan gave order for the practice of rain magic. This is a kind of sorcery carried out with various stones, the property of which is that when they are taken out, placed in water, and washed, wind, cold, snow, rain, and blizzards at once appear even though it is in the middle of summer. There was amongst them a Qangli̇ who was well versed in that art. In accordance with the command he began to practice it, and Tolui Khan and the whole army put on raincoats and for 3 days and nights did not dismount from their horses. The Mongol army [then] arrived in villages in the middle of Khitai from which the peasants had fled, leaving their goods and animals, and so they ate their fill and were clothed. Meantime the Qangli̇ continued to practice rain magic, so that it began to rain in the Mongols' rear and the last day the rain turned to snow, to which was added an icy wind. Under the effects of summer cold, such as they had not experienced in winter, the Khitayan army were disheartened and dismayed. Tolui Khan ordered [his] army to enter the villages, a unit of a thousand to each village, [and to] bring their horses into the houses and cover them up, since on account of the extreme severity of the wind and the icy blast it was impossible [to move about]. The Khitayan army, meantime, by force of necessity, remained out in the open country exposed to the snow and wind. For 3 days it was altogether impossible to move. On the fourth it was still snowing, but Tolui observed that his own army was well fed and rested and no harm had come to them or

---

102 1978a, p. 542.

> their animals from the cold, whereas the Khitayans, because of the excessive cold, were like a flock of sheep with their heads tucked into one another's tails, their clothes being all shrunk and their weapons frozen. He ordered the kettledrum to be beaten and the whole army to don cloaks of beaten felt and to mount horse. Then Tolui said: "Now is the time for battle and good fame: you must be men." And the Mongols fell upon the Khitayans like lions attacking a herd of deer and slew the greater part of that army, whilst some were scattered and perished in the mountains.[103]

Marco Polo mentions weather-magic twice in connection with the Mongols. First, he speaks about the Caraunas, who were a mixed race with a dominant Mongolian component, who belonged to the Chaghatai Ulus and made frequent raids on the eastern territories of Iran[104]:

> In this plain there are a number of villages and towns which have lofty walls of mud, made as a defence against the banditti, who are very numerous, and are called CARAONAS. This name is given them because they are the sons of Indian mothers by Tartar fathers. And you must know that when these Caraonas wish to make a plundering incursion, they have certain devilish enchantments whereby they do bring darkness over the face of the day, insomuch that you can scarcely discern your comrade riding beside you; and this darkness they will cause to extend over a space of seven days' journey.[105]

---

[103] Boyle 1971, pp. 36–7; Persian text Ali-zade (ed.) 1980, pp. 64–5.

[104] Pelliot (1959–1963–1973, i, pp. 183–96) has a lengthy commentary on the Caraunas.

[105] Yule 1921, i, p. 98. On dust storms as real meteorological phenomena, see Yule's note (pp. 105–6).

Marco Polo also speaks of the "crafty enchanters and astrologers" active at the court of the Mongolian Great Khan, Kubilai:

> But I must now tell you a strange thing that hitherto I have forgotten to mention. During the three months of every year that the Lord resides at that place, if it should happen to be bad weather, there are certain crafty enchanters and astrologers in his train, who are such adepts in necromancy and the diabolic arts, that they are able to prevent any cloud or storm from passing over the spot on which the Emperor's Palace stands. The sorcerers who do this are called TEBET and KESIMUR, which are the names of two nations of Idolaters. Whatever they do in this way is by the help of the Devil, but they make those people believe that it is compassed by dint of their own sanctity and the help of God.[106]

The kind of weather-magic described here by Marco Polo is distinctly different from all the instances previously discussed. The aim of weather-magic in this case was to avert bad weather—clouds and storms—from over the Great Khan's residence. However, this was clearly not a genuine Mongolian practice, since it was performed by some Tibetan and Kashmiri sorcerers—a testimony to the extraordinary degree of religious tolerance at Kubilai's court noted by Marco Polo.[107]

To sum up: both Mongolian and non-Mongolian historical sources recount examples of the Mongols' making use of weather-magic in warfare in the thirteenth and fourteenth centuries. The essence of the ceremony is related by Juvaini: certain stones were placed in water and washed. Rashīd al-Dīn, who may have relied on Juvaini, appended a brief, but precise, description of weather-magic following the Naiman story from the *Secret*

---

[106] *Op. cit.*, i, 301.
[107] Cf. Grousset 1970, p. 297.

History, an explanation, clearly, for the benefit of the non-Mongolian reader:

> *Jadāmīshī* was performed to bring forth snow and wind. *Jadāmīshī* means that incantations are recited, different kinds of stones are placed in water, and that abundant rains will come.[108]

According to the *Altan Tobči*, *ǰada* was used by the Mongols at the end of the Yüan Dynasty (1280—1367/68) when, pursued by the Chinese, they retreated to their home country. The Mongols used weather-magic to raise a great storm in which the bulk of the Chinese army and their horses were frozen to death.[109]

Additional light is shed on these descriptions by Chinese sources from the time of the Yüan Dynasty, which identify the rain-stones—called *cha-ta*, the Chinese rendering of Mo. *ǰada*—as bezoar.[110] The "various stones", thus, that Juvaini and Rashīd al-Dīn speak of the Mongols as using in their rain-making practices might well have originated in the stomachs and intestines of their animals.

---

[108] *Īshān jadāmīshī karda būdand, tā barf va dama bar āyad, va maʿnā-yi jadāmīshī ān-ast, kī afsūn-ī bar mī-khwāhand va sanghā az anvāʿ dar āb mī-nihand, va bārandagī bisyār mī-bāshad* (Berezin 1868, p. 205).

[109] Bawden 1955, pp. 151–2, Mongolian text p. 65.

[110] Laufer 1919, p. 527; Franke 1956, p. 97.

THE TIMURIDS AND AFTER

Let us now return to our review of Turkic weather-magic, and look at the period following the Mongol conquest. As shall be seen, after the thirteenth century, weather-magic took different forms at different levels of Turkic society.

Weather-magic as a tactical device in warfare was still current among the Turks, particularly among the Timurids, where it was a kind of family tradition passed on from father to son, as among the Khwārazmshāhs. The first time that weather-magic occurs in connection with Timur himself was at the beginning of his career, in the "Battle of the Mire"[111] fought on the right bank of the Syr Darya between Chināz and Old Tashkent in 1365:

> In this order they[112] attacked the enemy, but in pursuance with the words: "It is an evil day for you when you boast of your own strength or numbers," they were not spared from an unexpected punishment, for the army of Jatah, which, in spite of its superiority in numbers, had been defeated at Kaba Matan, now that they found their opponents exceeded in numbers, had recourse to magic, and sought aid from the Jadah stone, which possessed supernatural properties.
>
> [Verses]:
> The army of Jatah had no strength for the fight,
> So they sought help from the magic stone.
> With the stone of Jadah, who was a magician[113],
> They filled the world with wind and rain,
> The clouds roared with thunder and the winds howled.
> A thunderbolt fell upon the earth.

---

[111] Pe. *lāy* 'black viscous mud' (Steingass 1892, p. 1114).

[112] *I.e.* Timur and his allied troops.

[113] This must be a mistake, as the name of the magician the form **jadačï* could be expected.

> Although the sun was in Orion, a host of dark clouds suddenly filled the sky. The thunder resounded and the lightning flashed. The elements rushed out from the ambush of destiny into the open plain of the ether, and the thunderclaps re-echoed round the azure vault of heaven. The arrows of lightning were shot out, in all directions, from the bow of the thunder-clouds, and the rain shot down its whistling darts. It seemed as if the Fates had again become a prey to the love of rebellion and confusion. Such a quantity of water descended from the eyes of the stars, that the Deluge seemed to occur a second time. And the voice of Noah was again heard to pray for the cessation of the waters of heaven.[114]

Timur lost this battle, and Mīrzā Muḥammad Haidar, the author of the *Tarīkh-i Rashīdī*, who was related to the Timurids, tries his best to find excuses. Timur's defeat is attributed to the magical *ǰada*-stone used by the enemy, who were actually of Mongolian stock. At any rate, though it was the Mongolian *ǰätäs* that used weather-magic against Timur's army, the belief that it was effective must have been current also among the Turks. Otherwise Mīrzā Muḥammad Haidar would have had to find some other explanation for the great conqueror's defeat.

In 1451, certain Uzbeks in the army of Timur's great-grandson, Sultan Abū Saʿīd, performed weather-magic by means of the *yada*-stone, and brought on cold, snow and rain in an attempt to alleviate the suffering of the men and their animals as they crossed the Hunger Steppe.[115]

It is not known who it was that worked the weather-magic in the course of the march across the Hunger Steppe. However, Ẓahīr al-Dīn Bābur, Abū Saʿīd's grandson, mentions a certain ʿAlī Dōst Toghay who served Sulṭān Abū Saʿīd and occasionally did weather-magic, in Bābur's words "performed the prayer of weather-magic (*yadačïlïq duʿāsïnï qïlur*

[114] Elias (ed.)—Ross (transl.) 1895, pp. 32–3.
[115] Barthold 1956–1958, ii, p. 167.

idi)". ʿAlī Dōst Toghay was one of ʿUmār Shaikh Mīrzā's Tümen begs. He was also related to Bābur's family on the mother's side.[116] Bābur likewise mentions a high-ranking person in his retinue, Khwājaki Mullā-i Sadr, who had been appointed Keeper of the Seal (*muhrdār*) by ʿUmar Shaikh. Khwājaki Mullā-i Ṣadr practised both falconry and weather-magic (*quščïlïq vä yadačïlïq häm bilür idi*), as Bābur remarks in the account of his death near the Zerafshān River in 1497.[117]

The use of *yadačïlïq* is recorded by Bābur in his description of the Uzbek stratagem in a clash at Jām in Khurāsān in 1528. The Safavid army was under the personal command of Ṭahmāsp I:

> Here-upon the Aūzbegs, with entire disregard of their opponents, left their counsels at this: — "Let all of us sulṭāns and khāns seat ourselves in Mashad; let a few of us be told off with 20,000 men to go close to the Qīzīl-bāsh camp and not let them put head out; let us order magicians to work their magic directly Scorpio appears (*yadačïlarġa buyurmïz kim yada qïlġaylar*); by this stratagem the enemy will be enfeebled, and we shall overcome."[118]

As a matter of fact, the *yadačïlïq* failed to work, and the Uzbeks were defeated. The Persian victory was achieved through the use of artillery which Ṭahmāsp's amīrs had adopted from the Ottoman Turks.[119] The type of warfare used by the Safavid army in the battle of Jām marked the beginning of a new epoch in Central Asian history, warfare for which the Uzbek *yadačis* were no match.

---

[116] Beveridge (transl.) 1905, p. 27, Chaghatai text Ilminski 1857, p. 18.

[117] Beveridge (transl.) 1905, p. 67, Chaghatai text Ilminski 1857, p. 49.

[118] Beveridge (transl.) 1905, p. 623, Chaghatai text Ilminski 1857, p. 450.

[119] Roemer 1986, p. 236.

Bābur also recounts a more peaceful use of weather-magic in connection with an excursion he made to Lamghān in 1520. As it was raining heavily, he taught a *ṭilism*—a magical text written to avail against enchantment—to a certain Mullā ʿAlī Khān who, according to Bābur's instructions, wrote it down on four pieces of paper, and suspended them in the four directions. As soon as he did so, the rain stopped, and the air began to clear.[120] In this case, the aim of the weather-magic was to stop the rain. This is clearly weather-magic of another type, and the Turkic word *yada* does not occur in this context.

Weather-magic thus survived as a current belief among the Central Asian Turks into the fourteenth and fifteenth centuries. Among the Timurid rulers, three members of the dynasty were even personally involved to some degree in the performance of weather-magic.

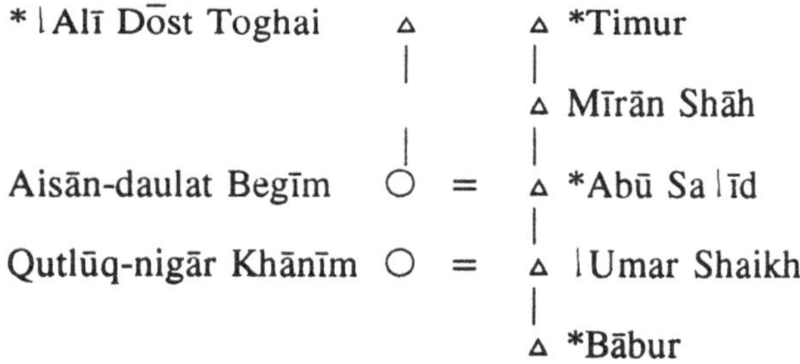

Figure 3. Members of the Timurid dynasty involved in weather-magic (marked with an asterisk)

Otherwise, weather-magic continued to be a part of Turkic culture mostly in the form of scholarly tradition, and it also found its way into the Turkic (Chaghatai) literature. It was, primarily, the Islamized ancestral legend of the Turks, *i.e.* the story of the sons of Japheth and the rain-stone,

---

[120] Beveridge (transl.) 1905, p. 422–3, Chaghatai text: *bir ṭilismi bilür idim. Mullā ʿAlī Khanġa örgätim. Tört parča kāġädgä bitip tört ṭarafqa astï. ušul zamān yamġur turup havā ačïlmaq bunyād qïldï* (Ilminski 1857, p. 322–3).

that was adopted and further developed. Mīrkhwānd, a historian of the Timurid era, relates the story in his universal history as follows:

> Some have said that Japheth became a prophet, appointed by the Almighty. When Noah took leave of him at the foot of Mount Jūdī[121], and sent him towards the north and the east, over which he had been appointed, Japheth requested his father to teach him a prayer by means of which he might procure rain at any time. Noah complied, and, after having turned towards the Lord of Glory, Gabriel brought in response to his request the ineffable Name, which Noah carved on a stone and gave to Japheth. It is called "rain-stone," but the Turks have named it *jada-taš*.
>
> When Japheth left the "Forum of the eighty," he travelled for a long time until he arrived at the limits of his empire, where he pursued a nomadic life and established good customs. When his progeny had greatly increased, he removed his goods and chattels to the abode of perpetuity [*i. e.* he died]. Some say that he laid the foundation of one of the great cities of China in his dominions. It is related that the Bestower of all good gifts had granted to him eleven sons—namely—Chīn, Saqlab, Kumārī, Turk, Khalaj, Khazar, Rūs, Sadsān, Uzz, Bāraj and Manshaj—each of whom he married to one his own daughters, commanding them to cultivate the land, and to multiply the number of the worshippers of God.
>
> Turk, the son of Japheth, his successor, and the most intelligent of his sons, strenuous, upright, and sagacious, also called Japheth Oghlān, was the first who explored those regions. He arrived at a place called *Selūk*, where he found a lake with warm water, pleasant springs, and numberless prairies. The locality suited Turk extremely well. He settled

---

[121] *I.e.* the Mount Ararat.

therein, erected houses built of wood and grass; after some time he invented tents by sewing together hides of sheep and of other animals. He was a just and excellent king, cared unceasingly for the well-being of his subjects, and the servants of God—whose name be exalted—reposed in tranquillity under the shadow of his protection. The Bestower of all good gifts presented him with children worthy of himself. One of these, Fundūk by name, who was addicted to hunting, one day roasted and consumed some of the game he had slain, when suddenly a piece of meat slipped from his hand into saline ground. On taking up the meat again he found it to be very savoury; he accordingly began to salt his victuals, and this custom originated from that day among the Turks, who are his descendants.

Khazar travelled in the north, and when he arrived on the *Ätil*[122] he was so pleased that he built a city, where his sons introduced in the world the art of catching foxes, of the skins whereof they made clothes, according to the instructions of their father, during whose lifetime one of his sons happened to die. For a long time he knew not what to do with the corpse. As, however, Japheth, with some of his adherents, had perished in the sea, he kindled fire, which is antagonistic to water, and threw the body into it, causing his followers to play on musical instruments and sing during the act of cremation; and it is said that this blamable habit is still flourishing in that country. It is said that his descendants followed bees until they arrived in the cavities of mountains, where they found honey, of which they prepared sweetmeats.

After some time Rūs arrived in the vicinity of the country of Khazar, and sent to him a messenger for the purpose of asking permission to settle in the realm. Khazar

---

[122] Spelt *Amut.

received the envoy with compliments, and presented his master with several oases possessing a good climate with a fertile soil. When each of the children of Japheth had taken up his abode in a separate region, his son, Uzz went to the outskirts of the country of Bulghār, constructed edifices, and settled there. Uzz was a cunning and deceitful nature, who carried on great wars against his brother Turk: the reason of which was that when Japheth got drowned in some sea, the stone which he had received through Noah for the purpose of obtaining rain had fallen into the hands of Uzz; but as every one of the brothers coveted that stone, Uzz made use his cunning disposition, and, procuring a false stone, which resembled the true one, he carved the ineffable Name on it. In order to settle the dispute who should obtain the stone, the brothers drew lots, and Turk having won, Uzz was compelled to surrender it. He did so, but it was the fabricated stone. Turk entertained no suspicion, and, joyfully accepting it, never tried it till several years afterwards, when he stood in need of rain. He produced the just-mentioned stone, but his asking for rain was of no use, wherefore he became convinced that Uzz had deceived him. He accordingly collected an army, which mountain and dale were too small to hold, and hastened to meet and to fight his brother for the purpose of recovering the original stone. Uzz was likewise ready with numerous troops, and sent his eldest son, Yabghū[123], who was decorated with the ornaments of valour and bravery, to combat Turk. A sanguinary battle ensued, in which Yabghū was killed. Turk returned, but it is said that enmity subsists till this day between the descendants of the two families.[124]

---

[123] spelt BGhWR.

[124] Rehatsek 1891, pp. 92–4.

In Mīrkhwānd's narrative, Japheth had eleven sons; their numbers increased by the addition of eponymous names (Sadsān, Bāraj and Manshaj) generated by misreadings. At any rate, in this account, too, the rivals were Uzz (Oghuz) and Turk (see *Fig.* 2).

Mentions of weather-magic in the *Bāburnāma*, that masterpiece of Chaghatai prose, have already been considered. However, the *yada taši* occurs as an allusion also in a poem by ʿAlīshīr Navāʾī, a Chaghatai classic, in his *Favāyidu'l-Kibar* cycle, "The Uses of Old Age"[125]:

> Ò échanson! de ce que le sang, lorsqu'il il touche
> la pierre à pluie, provoque une averse;
> de même, lorsque ta lèvre de rubis est imprégnée
> de vin, mes larmes pleuvent à torrent.[126]

Interestingly, Navāʾī's typical Ṣūfī poetical allusion reveals more about the technique of performing weather-magic than the references found in Bābur: the *yada taši* was stained in blood, as we have already seen in the *Ta'rīkh-i Fakhru'd-Dīn Mubārakshāh*.

From the post-Timurid period, we shall quote here only one reference to weather-magic from the scholarly tradition. Abū'l-Ġāzī Bahādur Khan, himself a descendant of the Uzbek dynasty, relates an event in his *Shäjärä-i Türk*, "The Origins of the Turks", when weather-magic was employed by Tolui's army against the Chinese (Jürchen):

> Tolui Khan had the news that they were in great straits. He conceived, that he should order the weather magicians (*yadačïlar*) to perform weather-magic (*yada*). So the weather-magicians were practicing their art during three days and nights, while on a hot summer day it began to

---

[125] Pavet de Courteille 1870, p. 519–20; Radloff 1888–1911, iii, p. 4; Inan 1954, p. 162, etc.

[126] *yada tašïġa qan tegäč yaġïn yaġqan-dek, ey, sāqī/ yaġar yamġur-dek äškim čūn bolur laʿliŋ šarābālūd* (Pavet de Courteille, *op. cit*).

snow and rain. It became so cold, that lots of men were unable to take their hands out of their bosoms. Tolui Khan saw that the Chinese army got entirely exhausted by the cold, so he issued the command to attack the Chinese army by a cavalry charge from the enemy's flank. So the Moġuls launched a cavalry charge and defeated the Chinese. Out of 100,000 men, one thousand fled and thus escaped, all the others were massacred.[127]

Beyond doubt, Abū'l-Ġāzī has relied on Rashīd al-Dīn for his Tolui story. Thus, while the *Shäjärä-i Türk* is part of the scholarly tradition, mostly on linguistic grounds we can assume that Abū'l-Ġāzī was also otherwise familiar with the nature of weather-magic: in his Chaghatai text, weather-magic is called *yada*. Had he followed Rashīd al-Dīn's text without personal knowledge of this practice, he would have kept his source's original wording, which is *ǰadāmīshī*.

Abū'l-Ġāzī's *Shäjärä-i Türk* is the last historical work to contain a specific reference to the use of weather-magic. The Central Asian Turkic and Mongolian literary epics of subsequent ages built on the above-discussed "historical" events will be considered in the next chapter.

---

[127] The Chaghatai text: *Toluy χan χabardār boldï, kim iš mäšgul bolup turur. fikr qïldï taqï yadačïlarga ḥukm qïldi yada qilïnglar tip. yadačïlar üč kičä kündüz yada qïldïlar. yaznïng isig künidä qar birlän yaġmur yaġa bašladï. andaġ savuq boldï, kim küp kiši qulïnï quyïnïdïn čïqara bilmädi. Toluy χan kördi, kim χatay läškäri savuqdïn ʻāǰiz bolup turur. čäriginä ḥukm qïldï, kim χatāy läškärigä äṭrāfïndïn at salïnglar tip. moġullar äṭrāfïndïn at saldïlar taqï χatay läškärini basṭïlar. yüz ming kišidin beš ming kiši qačïp qurtuldï, özgäläri hämä qatl ʻām boldï* (Desmaisons 1871–1874, i, p. 138).

THE OTTOMAN TURKS

Though the Ottoman Turks are beyond the scope of the present study, it seems appropriate to consider some of the Ottoman Turkish sources that have preserved some accounts of Inner Asian weather-magic.

A number of the narratives of Turkic weather-magic quoted above gained currency in the Ottoman Empire as parts of treatises on mineralogy. Tīfāshī's stories on the peculiarities of the rain-stones and their use at the court of the Khwārazmshāhs were copied by Bailak ibn Muḥammad al-Qibǰāqī in his *Kanz al-Tijār fī ma'rifat al-Aḥjār* "A Merchants' Treasury of Knowledge on Stones" written in 1282[128], and the same texts can also be found in the *Risāla-i Jawāhir* "A Treatise on Precious Stones", the work of the Persian scholar, Muḥammad ibn Manṣūr Shīrāzī.[129] These mineralogical treatises were popular in the Ottoman Empire. Several copies of each have been preserved in Turkish libraries[130], and at the turn of the seventeenth and eighteenth centuries, some narratives about rain-stones were translated into Ottoman Turkish by Şâban Şifaî Efendi, the renowned physician. His *Risale-i şifâiyye fi beyani enva'-i ahcar* "A Treatise on the Different Kinds of Medicinal Stones" has been preserved in various manuscripts[131]. In the following, the last part of Şâban Şifaî Efendi's work, entitled *Hacer-i Berf-ü Baran* "The Snow- and Rain-Stone" will be quoted[132]:

---

128 Ullmann 1972, p. 128.

129 *Op. cit.*, p. 136

130 *Op. cit.*

131 Ünver 1953, p. 78.

132 The English translation is based on Ünver's edition (1953, pp. 79—84) of the Antalya Ms. and Tanyu's edition (1968, pp. 223—30) of the facsimile of another Ms. kept in the Nuruosmaniye Kitaplığı (No. 3544 Mikrofilim A. 1125).

Abū'l-Barakāt Nīshābūrī[133], Nāṣir Ṭūsī, the wise Tīfāshī, Manṣūrī and other reliable scholars tell curious stories and odd accounts of this stone, and credit them, as they themselves have heard these stories from reliable persons. The Turks call this stone *yada taš*. It has different kinds of strange qualities. Some of them are earth-coloured, with white and red spots, while some others are spotless white. Some other stones are red, like clotted blood, and again some others are of various colours.

Abū'l-Barakāt says, "I have seen several kinds of the above-described stones in the treasury of the Sulṭān." Some great men claim that it is a mineral. It is said that it can be found in the provinces of China (Khatāy and Tamghach). There is controversy over the claim that it occurs in the stomachs of some pigs. Otherwise, there lives a kind of wild-duck in the provinces of China, and in the eastern regions of Iran, that has red wings and a bulky body. In Persian it is called *surkhāb*[134]. During the springtime these birds build their nests in shallow lakes. This stone can be found if one digs into the soil to the depth of two ells under the nests when the water recedes from these places during summertime. All the stones are brought to the treasury of the sovereign. This bird is also common in Egypt, where it is called *sammur*[135]. Boats are decorated with its feathers, but the peculiarities of this bird are not known there. The Turks agree that wherever the stone is used, its effect certainly appears in that place and its surroundings, and produces snow and rain. Some Turks know the peculiarities of this stone, and are skilled in their art to such a high degree that during the summer, [when the Sun is] in the

[133] The identity of Abū'l-Barakāt Nīshābūrī is not known to me.

[134] The ruddy goose (*Casarca ferruginea*).

[135] A corrupted form of *bashmur*.

constellation Leo, they can produce rain, snow, strong winds and other miraculous effects with that stone. They can conjure up snow and rain in one quarter of a town or a village, while producing sunshine and fine weather in other quarters. Some people say that there are different stones to produce rain, and again different ones to produce snow, hail, wind, dust-storms and changable weather. However, according to most narrators, all these are one and the same stone, that is, called *ḥajar al-maṭar* or *sang-i yada*. The initiates in this art can compound the appearance of these curious phenomena. This means that if some of these initiates come together in one place, and one practices his art to bring down snow, the second to bring down rain, and the third to bring down hail—thanks to the favour and graciousness of the Possessor of Omnipotence, the Majesty of God—the effects of their art appear simultaneously. In case there is only one initiate, he can produce only snow or rain, that is, only one of these curious phenomena. Some learned men say about these miraculous phenomena and the means of their production that they are known only to certain persons among the Turks. It is said that they are called *yadačï*[136], and that the stones do not exert their influence unless an incantation is recited. Some people say that the effectiveness of this stone is confined to Turkistān; in other regions it is ineffective. However, Ṭūsī contradicts them: "Wherever, in any region, this special stone is used, if someone wants [to produce] rain [by means of this stone], it rains. But you need someone who knows how to do it." Still, [Ṭūsī] does not explain the means and principles [of using the rain-stone]. Some simply put one of these stones into a bowl full of water or snow, and place it in a high place. Whatever is wished is fulfilled.

---

[136] Spelt **BT ḤRBY*. Ünver reads **yat hizbi*.

The late Tīfāshī firmly states that it takes a skilled person to use the stone. That wise man[137] confidently relates stories that he has heard from reliable persons. Tīfāshī was told of how an old Turk with an angry countenance had used the stone in the camp of one of the famous sultans of yore, the Khwārazmian Sulṭān Muḥammad Khān:

"That famous sovereign went to a campaign with innumerable soldiers during the days of summer. In a desert, all the people of the train, rich and poor, infantrymen and mounted soldiers greatly suffered a lot from the excessive heat and the heavy dust. The glorious Sulṭān gave orders to the man who kept this stone that the old man should use it in the way conforming to the principles [of its usage], so that the weather would, by the leave of Allah, be milder. The keeper of the stone, according to the order of the sovereign, summoned that old Turk. Being acquainted with them, I myself was present, and watched what he was doing. The old man uncovered his head. Having filled a bowl with water he placed it in front of himself. He also took three long reeds. He drove one reed into the ground on the right side of the bowl, the other on the left side, and he fixed the third reed to the upper ends of the other two above the bowl. Then he took a live snake of the same colour as the stone, and fixed it, hanging head down to the reed above the bowl, so that there was a distance of two ells between the head of the snake hanging down and the surface of the water. After that, he got two pieces of stone from the keeper of the stones, and put them into the water. After some time, he took the stones out, rubbed them one against the other, and then threw the stones against the two sides [of the bowl]. Then again he threw the stones into the water and

[137] Namely, Tīfāshī.

taking them out, rubbed them. Then he threw them again into the water. After having repeated this seven times, he took some water [out of the bowl], and sprinkled it on the ground. All the while the old man was bare-headed, his hair was disheveled and he looked angry. He murmured some words, raised his head towards the sky, and prayed for rain. He kept repeating this for two hours. Then suddenly, clouds appeared on the edges of the sky, and it began to rain heavily; the air cooled down, and the men and the animals were eased."

The narrator of the above story continues: "I had not conceived the wisdom of the Lord of the Universe, the Powerful and Glorious, his commands and the secrets He had entrusted on his creatures, so I remained in the company of the old man and watched him repeat the events described above several times. When I returned from the visit I had paid [the old man], I could not pass on account of the torrents caused by the abundance of rain. It is related that all this is the wisdom of God, may He be exalted. If someone who is engaged in this matter begins to practice his art at just any time, he will see a reversal of his fortune; his children and family will certainly be struck by misfortune, and in the end he will finish his life in poverty. Nevertheless, the favour of the sulṭān is generously bestowed on the practitioners of this art."

Besides Tīfāshī's account, reliable and well-known personalities have told another story as follows, "Still before Chenggis' conquest, the Khwārazmshāh Sulṭān Muḥammad marched against China (*Chīn*). As he neared this country, he got stuck in such heavy rain and snow that a lot of his soldiers were in peril of death. The sovereign understood that such bad weather could have been caused in that season of the year only with the use of the rain-stone, and he sent some of his men to the mountain near his camp. There two evil men were caught making rain, and they were brought into the presence of the sultān. The sovereign ordered the two scoundrels be wrapped into black felt and buried alive, and the weather immediately began to clear. The sovereign said, 'Had the two men who had caused the rain not been killed, the effects of their activities would have lasted longer, and they would have continued to produce snow, rain and flood.' The *sang-i yada* is one of the stratagems [used by] the kings of Transoxania. They bring on snow, rain and flood by means of the *yada*, and with the help of the *yadačï*s, and [thus] they become victorious over their enemies."

As told above, some persons themselves can produce effects peculiar to that stone, and if snow, rain or rainstorm is wanted, they can produce, even without spells and enchantments, the same effects that are otherwise produced by dipping that stone in water. Such a curious story is told [as follows]. In the old days, since there was a great need for rain in the town of Samarkand, that stone was put in a bowl full of water, and left at some place. A man called Ḥāfiẓ, not being aware of this, drank the water. At that very moment it began to rain, and did not cease to rain night and day. It was feared that not only the houses of Samarkand, but even some districts [around it] would be destroyed, and their inhabitants would perish. Finally, it was understood that this heavy rainfall had been caused by Ḥāfiẓ's drinking the water, and the wrongdoer was expelled from town. Then the rain stopped, but wherever Ḥāfiẓ went, the roads were blocked by torrents, and wherever he wanted to settle, it rained endlessly and so heavily that the local people were bewildered. In short, when the omens that had gone before Ḥāfiẓ were understood, the wrongdoer was driven away from the country, and the rain stopped. Anywhere he went, it rained. It was seen that his conduct was evil, thus he was expelled from Transoxania and Khurāsān, and could not remain in any place. Finally he took refuge in Egypt. Due to the blessedness of this country, his condition disappeared of itself. After some time, his heart, filled with love for his country, longed to go back to Samarkand. Still, he abandoned [the idea of going home] because he feared that his strange condition would return. After a long time, he finally did return, and was united with his family. His strange condition did not come back again, but, referring to that stone, his name became Ḥāfiẓ Yada.

It is related that the effects of the stone certainly do not appear if it is dipped into water by common people. As mentioned above, it is necessary to find skilled magicians (*sihirbâz*). It is said that some devotees of this practice bring on strange phenomena like snow, rain, and hail and strong wind by means of stones originating from animals, such as fish, or from the human urinary bladder. However, Naṣīr Ṭūsī's statement cannot be applied to some of these stones, and Muḥammad bin Zakariyyā' Abū-Bakr Rāzī's story of the mountain pass (*'aqaba*) is about these latter.

This great and reliable scholar says in his work, the *Kitāb al-Khawwāṣṣ*: "In Turkistan, between two countries, there is a mountain pass (*'aqaba*). Those who want to get through this mountain pass wrap felt on the feet of their riding and baggage animals, so that the hooves and shoes of the animals should not hit the stones of that dangerous road. If the hooves of the animals happen to strike against one of those stones, or an animal scrapes a stone in a tight pass, the sky immediately grows dark, clouds appear all around, and it begins to rain. If this happens during the winter, it rains so heavily that the torrents block the road. The people who pass this land take some of these stones, and carry them to the towns of Turkistan and to other places."

Muḥammad bin Zakariyyā.'s story, occurring in Naṣīr Ṭūsi's *Tansuqnāma[-i Ilkhānī]*, and in the works of other writers, is not peculiar to its author; there are many difficult passes in the land of Turkistan, and it is well known that travellers have seen the conditions [described above]. Furthermore, when passing those dangerous places, one is not allowed to shout, to speak loudly, to wash something, to relieve nature, and put black objects into water. It is related that in case any of these actions is done, it rains in summer, it snows in winter and a storm breaks out.

After having told of the above-mentioned circumstances, Abū'l-Barakat Nīshāpūrī asserts that according to reliable persons, these curious phenomena are well known and spread from mouth to mouth, and nobody denies them. Only the Master Abū'l-Rayḥān Bīrūnī ridicules these stories, "In my view, this kind of thing, that is, to rule over nature, cannot be done by man or by means of stones." His assertion, namely, that these narratives are fictitious stories (*ḥikâye*), may be due to the fact that the narratives of the above-quoted reliable scholars were not known to him. Additionally, there is no doubt that reports by eye-witnesses are also very common.

Abū'l-'Abbās Tīfāshī trained in science, credited the occurrence [of these phenomena], as it known from his *[Kitāb] Azhār al-Afkār [fī Jawāhir al-Aḥjar]*. Recounting narratives by reliable authors, he selected a verse from the Koran, from the sura of Joseph: '*Many are the marvels of the heavens and the earth; yet they pass them by and pay no heed to them.*'[138] The truth of this thing is known only to Allah, the Almighty.[139]

---

[138] The Koran 12:102.

[139] Ottoman Turkish text in Ünver 1953, pp. 79–84.

Şâban Şifaî Efendi's work is a compilation of several sources named at the beginning of the treatise. He seems to have followed most closely Abū'l-Barakāt Nishāpūrī, who had himself copied earlier authors. Most of the stories narrated by Şâban Şifaî Efendi have already been quoted above. The accounts of the *surkhāb*, the rain-making ceremony performed in the army of the Khwārazmshāh 'Alā' al-Dīn Muḥammad by an old Turk, and of the two weather-magicians buried alive ultimately derive from Tīfāshī's *Kitāb Azhār al-Afkār fī Jawāhir al-Aḥjar.* The narrative of the rain-stones in the mountain pass located in the land of the Karluks—without the Karluks being mentioned, however—can be traced to Muḥammad ibn Zakariyyā' al-Rāzī's lost *Kitāb al-Khawwāṣṣ*, preserved in al-Bīrūnī's *Kitāb al-Jamāhir fī Ma 'rifat al-Jawāhir*, and in Nāṣir Ṭūsī's *Tansuqnāma-i Ilkhānī.*[140]

However, Şâban Şifaî Efendi gives also an account which does not occur in any of the other sources, the story of Ḥāfiẓ-i Yada. The historical interpretation of the curious story of Ḥāfiẓ—who accidentally drank the water in which rain-stones were being soaked and himself became a "rain-magnet", and needed years to be "cured" of his strange condition—is, perhaps, that belief in weather-magic performed by means of rain-stones was introduced to Egypt by the Mameluk Kipchaks who originated from the territory of the Empire of the Khwārazmshāhs. Qibchāqī also mentions that it was a certain Azdemür of Cairo, who belonged to the entourage of a Khwārazmian amīr, who told him about the rain-stones.

Şâban Şifaî Efendi's treatise shows that stories of Turkic weather-magic performed by means of *yada*-stones were known in the Ottoman Empire, but only as part of the literary tradition. Since certain stones are put to similar use in contemporary Turkish rain-making ceremonies, it is tempting to see a historical connection between literature and this latter-day practice.[141] However, Acıpayamlı[142] rightly notes that though *yada-taşı* occurs in rain-making ceremonies among the Turks of Central Asia from

---

[140] See A Conspectus of the Early Islamic Sources.
[141] As did Boratav 1952, p. 1223 and 1978, p. 270.
[142] 1963–64, p. 230.

early times, the term has never occurred in the Turkish ways of making rain in Anatolia. There can be no doubt that the descriptions of rain-making ceremonies in the Ottoman Turkish literature are translations from Arabic, Persian and possibly Chaghatai originals. *Yada* is not a genuine Ottoman word. Though the linguistic aspects of *yada* will be discussed in depth in Chapter 3, it might be convenient to consider the status of *yada* in Ottoman Turkish at this point.

The *Tarama Sözlüğü*[143] gives two occurrences of *yada* in Ottoman Turkish texts: first, in the Persian construction *sang-i yada* in a seventeenth-century poem written by Nev'izade Atai, and second, in the Persian idiom *sang-i yada* in the Ottoman Turkish translation of Zamakhshahrī's *Muqaddimat al-Adab* made by Aydın'lı Ishak Hocası Efendi in Bursa some time before 1708. Therefore, Ottoman *yada* is an adoption from Persian, and its existence in the literary language is not connected with Anatolian Turkish rain-making beliefs and practices.

---

143 vi, p. 4189.

RECENT TURKIC AND MONGOLIAN BELIEFS

Our early sources on Turkic and Mongol weather-magic, reviewed in the previous chapter, have, for the most part, been accounts of various historical events. Sources for the Turkic and Mongol beliefs and rites of the eighteenth to the twentieth centuries are contemporary accounts of travellers and missionaries.

The Oghuz Turks

Turkish rain-making ceremonies have been the object of detailed studies.[144] Başgöz[145] has commented on the great variety of ceremonies performed in order to produce rain in Turkey. Some of these are common in the Balkans and in the Middle East as well, and bear a striking resemblance to the seasonal festivals of the Ancient Middle East. Acıpayamlı[146] gives a good overview of the rain-making rites and formulae used in Anatolia, where there are rites connected with stones, pebbles and sand. In Erzurum, children pick up stones from the ground; after prayers are said over them, the stones are thrown into water. In Savur, there is a collection of 7,000 small stones at the site where the *yağmur duası* 'supplication for rain' is said. Verses from the Koran are recited over each piece, and then they are thrown into water. Near

---

[144] Boratav 1952, 1978, Başgöz 1967 and Acıpayamlı 1963-64.

[145] *Op. cit.*

[146] 1963–64, p. 230.

Ankara, the supplicants for rain pick up 3—5,000 stones on the site of the ritual, pray over them, and put them into a sack tied with a piece of string to a peg driven into the ground on the riverside. Similar rituals are described for other parts of Turkey, too. In Tokat, 71,000 stones in a sack are immersed in the river before they are counted, and each one is blown at and licked. In the village of Bayındır, villagers carrying a sack full of stones go to a nearby spring abounding in water. The stones are poured out on the ground, and an animal is killed over them as a sacrifice. The animal's blood is poured on the stones while the *hoca* prays. Acıpayamlı[147] refers to several other examples from all over Turkey of stones or pebbles being picked up, counted, thrown into water, blown at, or licked.

The Azeri (nukhinskie tatarï) prayed by rivers and dropped a piece of stone into a bag after each prayer. Finally, they threw the bag filled with the stones into a dried-up riverbed.[148]

I myself have not found any description of Turkmen rain-making ceremonies originating from the territory of Turkmenistan, but Demidov[149] mentions a rain-maker from the Atabai clan of the Yomut Turkmen living along the Atrek River, who was still active at the beginning of the twentieth century. Terzibaşi[150], however, provides accounts of the rain-making ceremonies of the Turkmens living in Iraq, near Kerkük. At times of drought, the Turkmens, after fasting for three days, gather out of town, near a cemetery, or by a riverside. Following the *imam* or *hoca*, who wears his robe turned inside out, they say the *namaz*, without the *tekbir* (saying *Allahuekber*), however. Afterwards, the *imam* says the appropriate prayer, and the congregations answers *Âmin* 'amen'. During the ceremony, young children, who stand in the rear, keep shouting *Peygambere salâvât!* "May Allah bless the Prophet!". In the meanwhile,

---

147 1963, pp. 5—6, 13—7.

148 Collected by Malov (1947, p. 152) from an Azeri student of the Turkological Seminar in 1924.

149 1964, p. 8.

150 1976, pp. 305—10.

an animal is killed as a sacrifice, and its meat is distributed among the poor. The people break the fast by eating the food prepared at the site of the ceremony. During the rite, 70,000 pebbles are collected, certain verses of the Koran are recited over them, and then they are thrown into the river. In addition, the children find a horse's or donkey's skull, and burn it in the fire.

Another Turkmen rain-making ceremony performed in 1971, close to the burial place of an Islamic saint called Şıkh Nevrü, is reported from the district of Telâfer, near Mosul. The people assembled before the shrine killed an animal as a sacrifice, and then poured its blood into a stone-mortar. The Turkmens believe that this rite purifies the rain about to fall. Finally, Terzibaşı recounts a rain-making ceremony called *köse geldi*, "The *köse* has come". The *köse* is a young lad, with no beard or but a very sparse one, though his role can also be taken by a child. He paints his face black with soot taken from the bottom of a cauldron, fixes a piece of felt to his waist, fashions ears for himself from two old shoes, hangs a small bell called *kankavur* around his neck, and fixes a tail to his back. Then he hops and jumps about like an ass's foal in this disguise along the streets of the village. A troop of children follow him running and singing songs. They collect food from the houses, which they eat at the end. In the Chahār Mahal district, in the land of the Bakhtiyari[151] east of Isfahan, Iran, the following rite was performed in the case of drought: Some young people took stones in both their hands, and knocking them against one another, they sang *Hāy, hāy, Hārūneki! Ne istersen?* "What do you want?" asked one team of children; and the other team answered: *Su isterem!* "I want some water!". They were given some small presents at the gates of the houses.[152]

---

[151] The Bakhtiyari, of course, are Iranian. However, judging from the sample sentences, the quoted rite must have originated with some Oghuz tribes living in Iran.

[152] Massé 1938, p. 176.

THE TURKIC PEOPLES OF THE VOLGA REGION

Ashmarin[153] gives detailed descriptions of some Chuvash rain-making ceremonies, called *śumăr čükĕ* 'a prayer, an offering for rain'. The first, quoted by Ashmarin from an unknown source, was performed in the settlement of Čirkülĕ Ačča on the Śaval River in 1904 or 1906. Eggs, butter, porridge, bread and salt were collected from each house, and porridge with eggs prepared in a cauldron by the riverside. As soon as the food was ready, the participants at the rain-making ceremony waded into the water up to their knees. The cauldron was held by two elderly men in such a way that it was half in the water, and in the meanwhile, prayers were said. The elderly men wore long, loose overcoats (*aśam*) and held big caps under their arms. The sacrificial food was eaten, and afterwards, all the participants plunged into the water.

Another rain-making ceremony was reported to have been performed at the village of Katek. The food was prepared in a similar way, but at an open fireplace, rather than by the river.

Yet another instance of rain-making rite is said by an unknown source to have been performed at the settlement of Šĕrpü (Mami rayon, belonging to the Parish of Ačča). The adults told the children to collect flour, porridge, butter and eggs. While the porridge was prepared by the riverside, the children were sent off again to catch some young sparrows. Some of the fledgings were drowned in the river, others in the broth. Some herbs were collected and planted by the riverside. As soon as the food was ready, the elderly members of the community poured the food on the hillsides and the riverside. Afterwards, with their caps under their arms, they said prayers. Then, all the people, children and their parents, went to the place by the river where the food containing the drowned sparrows had been poured. Everybody wore black; white clothes were strictly prohibited. They ate the food they had brought along, and

153 1928–50, xii, pp. 237–8, under *śumăr čükĕ*.

afterwards, everybody plunged into the river and splashed in the water like ducks.

Malov[154] describes a Kazan Tatar ritual he observed in the village of Chukrï (Alanovo) in 1901. That summer, on a day of drought, the people left the village in the morning and gathered by the riverside. Porridge was prepared in cauldrons dug deep into the ground. The mulla recited verses from the Koran, and then the porridge was distributed among the participants at the ceremony. The people ate the porridge and went home. The same day, young people threw water at whomever they came across in the streets.

In rites of the Eastern Bashkir clans of Olo Katay, Saljïvït and Barïn-Tabïn, participants throw each other into the water, or splash water at each other.[155] The aim of the ceremony is to produce rain, and it somewhat resembles the Chuvash and Kazan Tatar rituals. However, there is another type of Bashkir weather-magic, aimed at producing rain and storm. This type differs from similar rites of the other two Turkic peoples of the Volga region, but shows similarities to some Kazak and Kirghiz rites to be discussed below.

In the Beloretskiy rayon of Bashkiria southeast of Ufa, a certain stone found in a secluded clearing in the forest is believed to possess the magical power of changing the weather. The Bashkirs visit the place only when they want to do weather-magic by means of that stone. Rain and storm can be raised even by touching it. It is the mulla's duty to perform the ceremony: a piece is split off from the stone, and thrown into a nearby river. The stone is called *kolon taš*, literally meaning 'colt-stone,'[156] or *yäy taš*[157] in Bashkir, the latter being misunderstood as

---

[154] 1947, p. 151.

[155] Inan (1954, pp. 164–5). Inan does not give his source, but his account is most likely based on his own experience, he himself being a Bashkir of the Olo Katay clan.

[156] See Bashk. *kolon* 'a colt, foal' (*BRS 1958*, p. 337).

[157] See Bashk. *yäy* 'summer' (*BRS 1958*, p. 337).

'summer-stone' in popular etymology. Some other rain-stones are said to be found in the heads of birds.[158]

The Central Asian Kipchak Turks

According to the beliefs of the Kirghiz,[159] weather can be changed or foreseen with the help of the *ǰay*-stone,[160] in the stomachs of sheep and cows. Alternately, a piece of ordinary stone the size of a finger can be transformed into *ǰay-taš* by forty days of prayer and a magical procedure performed in water. A lost rain-stone may cause harm. Whoever finds it may be struck by poverty, illness and death. Therefore, a rain-stone is always carefully guarded by its owner, who might even bury it in the ground when he feels his death coming. An exclusive class of magicians, called *ǰayčï*, specializes in doing weather-magic, though the *bakšï* have also been known to perform the duties of a weather-magician. The Kirghiz believe that a *ǰayčï*'s death is followed by heavy rainfalls. To stop the rains, an incision is made with the point of a knife in the weather-magician's stomach, some of his eyebrows and lashes are plucked out, and then the corpse itself is buried. A small fire is lit over the *ǰayčï*'s grave, and the torn out eyebrows and lashes are thrown among the flames. It is believed that the rain will stop when the smoke reaches the sky. If the weather-magician is buried without performing the necessary rituals, or he happens to die while it is raining or snowing, his corpse is disinterred somewhat later, and the appropriate ceremony is performed. In some cases, the *ǰayčï*'s body is not buried, but incinerated.

---

158 The above Bashkir data were collected by Dr. J. Torma in 1989, who kindly put his still unpublished material at my disposal.

159 Abramzon 1971, pp. 298–9, Bayalieva 1972, pp. 54–5.

160 This is the common Kirghiz word for the 'rain-stone' as found in anthropological publications. However, Yudakhin (1985, p. 210) gives *ǰada* 'the same as *ǰay*' and 'weather-magic', as well as *kara taš* 'id.', meaning literally 'black stone'.

Abramzon[161] quotes the following Kirghiz rain-making ceremony after Bogdanova: the *ǰayčï* says a spell forty times over forty withes, then he submerges them in water, and turns towards the four cardinal points repeating the spell forty times. He obtains a few clods of earth from a grave, and saying the spell forty times once again, throws the clods towards the sky. Finally, he himself dips into water, and while sitting in it, repeats the spell again forty times. Yudakhin[162] gives a relevant passage from a folklore text, presumably from a folk-tale: *Eldiyar kara taštï duvalap, suuga salïp kalmaktar ǰatkan ǰerge kar ǰaadïrïp, özdürü ǰatkan ǰerdi ǰarkïratïp ačïk kïlïp* "Eldiyar prayed over the *kara taš*[163], the rain-stone; he dived into water and [this way] he procured snow to the place where the Kalmuck were staying, while in the place where they themselves were he made the weather clear and bright." Clearly, the weather-magic ritual consists of a prayer said over the rain-stone, and its immersion into water. The magic was practiced as a "meteorological weapon" against the Kalmucks, the traditional enemy of the Kirghiz in their epics and folklore.[164]

We find a similar event in the Kirghiz heroic epic, the *Manas*, in the scene when Manas' forty knights clash with the Kalmucks. Terror-struck, the Kalmucks realize that a tempest has been sent over them by Manas' companion, Almambet:

> If I look back,
> I cry out in fear:
> It is a dappled cloud, and a grey snow-storm there,
> And it looks like rain,

---

[161] 1971, pp. 298–9.

[162] 1971, pp. 298–9.

[163] The same as ǰay *taš*.

[164] Yudakhin (*op. cit.*) also cites another passage: *ǰay taštï kölge urdu — deyt, ǰay dubasïn küböröp, ǰaylap* ... 'It is said he threw the *ǰay*-stone into a lake, and murmuring the prayer of *ǰay*, he did weather-magic...'

On the other side, fog is hanging over the mountains,
This is weather-magic, done by Almambet.[165]

He who produces the clouds, the rain and the fog is called *jayči*[166], but the form *ǰadačï* also occurs in the epic with the same meaning.[167]

Weather-magic is seen again to be used in warfare in a Kirghiz folktale edited by Potanin.[168] A Kirghiz youngster helps the Kirghiz army to cross the Le (Ili) River by freezing its waters—he sits by the riverside and prays.

As noted, the Kirghiz differentiate between two rain-stones: those transformed from "ordinary" pieces of stone, and others found in the stomachs of animals. We find the same duality in the case of the Kazak rain-stones. For the first kind, I could find only a short reference in Valikhanov[169]: the Kazaks believe that rain and storm can be produced by means of the *ǰaytasï*, that is, the 'thunderbolt [gromovoy kamen']'. The other kind of *ǰaytasï* occurs in the Kazak epic poem *Er Köksü*, where the hero's son, Er Kosai, marching across the desert, meets five lads sore afflicted with hunger and thirst, who ask Er Kosai for help:

Sprachen die fünf Jünglinge, die bei ihm waren:
Unsere Seele Er Kosai,
Unser Leben Er Kosai,
Schon lange dursten wir,
Schon lange ertragen wir Unglück,
Was soll man dagegen thun?

---

165 *Anïn artïn karasam/ač kïykïrïk, kuu süröön/ala bulut, kök burgak/astï ǰagï bolgon ǰaan/arï četi ǰöö tuman/Almambettin ǰayï eken.* (Yunusaliev 1958, p. 287).

166 *Op. cit.*, p. 288, and elsewhere.

167 *Op. cit.*, p. 289.

168 1917, p. 67.

169 1953, p. 160.

Unser Magen ist hungrig.
Da wir nach Wasser dürsten,
Da wir nach Speise hungrig sind,
Wie sollen wir dem abhelfen?
Als die fünf Jünglinge so gesprochen,
Als Kosai ihre Rede gehört,
Den durstenden Menschen,
Den hungrigen Menschen
Will ich Wasser zum Trinken geben,
Will ich Speise für den Hunger geben,
In meinem Bogen-Köcher
Sind fünf Stücke Baursak[170],
Bei meinem gelben Pferde mit hängenden Ohren,
Unter seinem Bauche
Ist ein *ǰaydïŋ tasï*[171]
Die in seinem Köcher befindlichen
Fünf Baursak nahm er,
Gab sie alle fünf,
Die Fünf nahmen sie vor sich aufs Pferd
Und assen die fünf Baursak.
Den unter des gelben Pferdes mit hängenden Ohren
Bauche befindlichen
ǰaydïŋ tasï nahm er,
Ihn schwenkend, warf er ihn zur Erde,
Vom Himmel regnete es,

---

[170] *baursaq* 'kleine in Hammelfett gebratene Teigstücke (Lieblingsspeise der Kirgisen [*i.e.* Kazak A. M.]' (Radloff 1888–1911, iv, c. 1433).

[171] *ǰaydïŋ tasï*: Radloff translates 'ein Blitzstein (Belemnit?)': see also his *Wörterbuch*... Kaz. *ǰay* 'der Blitz's (1888–1911, iv, c. 2).

Von diesem Wasser tranken sie.[172]

As can be seen, the rain-stone (*ǰaydïŋ tasï*) lay hidden under the liver of Er Kosai's horse (*salpaŋ qulaq sar'attïŋ baurunüŋ astïnda ǰaidïŋ tasï bar ekän*) "There was a rain-stone under the liver of the flop-eared yellow horse."[173] When he wants to summon rain, that is where Er Kosai gets the rain-stone (*salpaŋ quluq sar'attïŋ baurunuŋ astïnda ǰaydïŋ tasïŋ alïptï*). This rather vague poetic expression appears to refer to the fact that the *ǰaydïŋ tasï* actually came from under a horse's liver. If so, the rain-stone has the same twofold meaning: 'a certain mineral', and 'a bezoar' as seen above in the case of the Kirghiz.

THE TURKIC PEOPLES OF TURKESTAN

Around Tashkent and Bukhara, the practice of producing rain with the help of the rain-stone was combined with Islamic rites. Dingel'shtedt[174] gives an amazing story which tells how rain-making related to agriculture. The highlanders living among the mountains had non-irrigated cultivated fields, and as their crop depended on precipitation, they clearly prayed for rainfall. On the other hand, the fields of the Sart population were irrigated; they needed no rain. In fact, rain could even have done harm to their crops. There was, thus, a kind of curious rivalry for the favour of

---

[172] Radloff 1870, ii, pp. 121–2, Kazak text i, pp. 95–6.

[173] Radloff (*op. cit.*) translates: 'Bei meinem gelben Pferde mit hängenden Ohren/Unter seinem Bauche/Ist ein Blitzstein (Belemnit?)'.It seems that Radloff did not understand this passage properly, and he had the other meaning of *ǰay* 'der Blitz' in mind. Inan (1954, p. 164), however, gives an accurate translation: 'Er Kosay, uzun kulaklı sarı atının ceğerlerinin altından cay taşı (yad taşı) çekip çıkardı.'

[174] 1893, p. 168.

the Heavens between the cultivators of the irrigated and the non-irrigated fields. The year of 1869 was especially dry, and a great many crops withered. Also, there were quick showers, particularly harmful to the irrigated crops. News spread among the Sart population that these showers had been produced by the learned Kirghiz[175] mullas with the help of the *yada-taš*.[176] The Sarts even asked the local authorities for permission to organize official prayers to stop the rain.

Logofat[177] refers rather vaguely to the *yad[a]*-stone in his half-fictitious travelogue: the Uzbeks seek for it in the mountains of Khazret-Sultan, near the Qizil-Darya. The stone can be found in caves and on rocks of difficult access. The magic stone can be recognized by the beams of light emanating from the ground where it lies hidden. Anyone wearing such a stone around his neck cannot be defeated in battle. Serpent's or scorpion's stings can be cured by placing the stone on the wound. The owner of the *yad[a]*-stone who also knows the appropriate spell can become invisible. There is no reference, however, to rain-making in connection with the *yad[a]*-stone.[178] In Bukhara, the Naqshbandi dervishes prayed over seven pebbles which were thrown into a river at times of draught[179].

The earliest account of Eastern Turki (New Uighur) and of Mongol (Torgut and Ölöt) weather-magic, is the *Hsi-yü wen-chien lu* written in 1777 by Ch'i-shih-yi, a Manchu civil servant residing in Sinkiang at the end of the eighteenth century[180]. The natives of

---

[175] In the original, "Kazak".

[176] Though it occurs in connection with the Kirghiz, this Turkic form can only be the name for the 'rain-stone' used by the Sarts (Uzbeks); the Kirghiz form would be *ǰay*. Apart from the corrupted variant given by Logofat (see below), this is the only occurrence of the word *yada* known in Uzbek.

[177] 1913, pp. 513–4.

[178] Logofat gives the form *yad-taš* in the Russian text; it can only be a corrupted form of *yada-taš*.

[179] Gordlevskiy 1934, pp. 155–6.

[180] Pelliot 1960, pp. 34, 87, note 251; see also notes 94–97.

Turkistan, he tells us, use the *yada-taš*, that is the bezoar, for making weather-magic. The *yada-taš* is as hard as stone: its colours are blue, yellow, white, green and blackish. *Yada*-stones of various sizes can be found in the stomachs of cows and horses, in the tails of lizards, and in the heads of wild boars. Those found in stomachs are the most effective. When the Turkis pray for rain, they fix the bezoar to a withe, and rain ensues. If it is clear weather that is prayed for, the stone is put into a small bag fixed to a horse's tail. If cool weather is necessary, the stone is put into a small bag and fixed to the weather-maker's belt. There are special prayers to be recited. The *aχuns*[181], when they pray for rain, fix the bezoar to a withe and hold it over their heads all the while they are praying. Those who prepare for a long journey during the summer buy a bezoar, and give it to the *aχun*, who weaves a net of black horse's hair, and, reciting a spell over the bezoar, wraps it in the net. If it is very hot during the journey, the traveller places the bezoar in his belt, and clouds would appear. If clear weather is needed, the bezoar is unwrapped and placed near a fire. The bezoar's failure to be effective is attributed to the past sins of the weather-maker.[182]

Another account of Turki and Mongolian weather-magic in Sinkiang was written by ʿAbdu'l-Karīm Bukhārī in his description of Central Asian lands appended to his *History of Central Asia*. Bukhārī's account dates from the beginning of the nineteenth century:

> Thourfan est situé sur la limite de Kachgar, et les villes de Qamil et de Soutsheou sont les premières villes de la frontière de Chine: entre Thourfan et ces deux dernières villes se trouve un désert d'une étendue de quarante journées de marche; il n'y a aucun endroit cultivé, mais on y trouve de l'eau. Ce désert était autrefois peuplé et

[181] See *aχun* 'a religious functionary, a theologian' (Nadzhip 1968, p. 23). The word is a loan from New Persian, see *akhwānd* 'tutor, master, preacher' (Steingass 1892, p. 26).

[182] Iakinf 1826, p. 214.

cultivé, mais Djenguiz, les empereurs de Chine et les chefs Qalmaq l'ont entièrement dévasté; c'est une plaine parfaitement unie. On ne peut le traverser en hiver, a cause de la terreur qu'inspirent les Qalmaq; car ces tribus, qui sont nomades, viennent s'y établir pendant la mauvaise saison. Pour ce motif. les caravanes ne s'y aventurent que pendant l'été. On provoque la pluie avec la pierre de yèdèh; cette pluie rafraîchit la température et permet de continuer son chemin. On franchit ainsi une route de vingt journées de marche; après ces vingt journées, la tempèrature est moins élevée et on n'a plus besoin de faire tomber de la pluie. Le yèdèh se trouve également en Crimée, chez les Tatares Nogaï; c'est une substance osseuse de la grosseur d'une noix et qui a la dureté de la pierre, on la trouve dans la tête de l'homme, du cochon, du cheval et d'autres animaux, mais il faut faire mille expériences avant de renconter la pierre véritable. Les gens qui font profession de connaître le yèdèh y inscrivent avec du sang de porc le nom de certains mauvais génies. Ils mettent aussi en usage certaines pratiques découvrir le yèdèh et ils s'en servent pour faire neiger, pleuvoir, et pour provoquer le froid. Les marchands qui se rendent en Chine prennent à leur solde un yèdèdjy, qui fait tomber la pluie et leur permet de marcher avec une température modérée. Pour conjurer les effets du yèdèh, il faut réciter le chapitre du Qoran «Ech chems»[183] et, avec la permission de Dieu, on annule son influence.[184]

Mir Izzet Ullah, who was dispatched in 1812 by the British on a preparatory tour to Central Asia, also speaks of the rain-stone when he describes Yarkand:

---

[183] *al-shams* 'the Sun', the 81th verse of the Koran.
[184] Schafer 1876, pp. 299—301.

> One of the curiosities of this country is the stone called Yedeh, a stone taken from the head of the cow or horse, by the virtue of which rain or snow may be produced. I had no opportunity of observing the fact, but the truth was attested by very many persons. The individuals who employ the stone are numerous; they are called Yedejis. The stone is to be smeared with the blood of some animal, and then thrown into water: a charm is read at the same time, upon which a strong wind springs up, and then rain and snow ensue. The virtues of the stone are confined to cold countries, and it would therefore be unavailing to transport it to the sandy districts of Hindustan, as Hariana and Bikaner. The truth of the story is known to God alone.[185]

However, our main source of information on New Uighur weather-magic are copies of certain *yadačï-kitab*s 'weather-magician's handbooks'. It seems to have been a special genre in Sinkiang[186] to note down the rites and prayers connected with weather-magic. Malov[187] obtained two such manuscripts on his journey to Sinkiang in 1913—15, one in Urumchi, which, according to its colophon[188], had been written my Memet Aziz-Akhun in the village of Kumbagh in the oasis of Keriya, the other originating from Aksu, and owned by Taira-Molla.

---

[185] Mir Izzet Ullah 1843, pp. 305—6.

[186] Dr. G. Jarring kindly informed me in a letter dated 8th December, 1989, that he has a still unpublished fragmentary copy of another *yadačï-kitab* which he acquired in Kashghar in 1923.

[187] 1947, p. 151.

[188] Malov, *op. cit.*, p. 158.

Malov[189] gives only the Russian translations of the two *risāles*, that is, of the two descriptions of rain-making ceremonies. The texts clearly show Islamic influence: for example, the introductory part of the text tells us that knowledge of *yadačïlïq*, 'the art of weather-magic', comes from Allah, and was revealed to Adam by the Archangel Gabriel. Before the ceremony, we read, the ritual ablution is obligatory; the appropriate prayers are to be recited from the Koran. The *yada*, 'rain-making ceremony', is performed by means of a dappled blue, yellow or reddish coloured *yada-taš* '*yada*-stone' found in the intestines of animals, such as boars, horses, goats, or even snow-leopards or lizards. There are certain indications of there being a *yada*-stone in an animal. If, for example, a horse crosses rivers during the winter without stopping to drink, there is a *yada*-stone in its intestines. The best kind of rain-stone can be recognized by the cracking sound it gives, when cast into water. When the magical power of the *yada*-stone begins to wane, it should immediately be dipped in blood, or given to a red cock to swallow. After three days the cock can be killed, and the revitalized stone regained from its intestines. The same result can be obtained by giving it to an old he-goat to swallow. After an hour or so, the goat can be slaughtered and the *yada*-stone taken from its stomach. The stone is to be put on a plate, a red and a white cock killed over it, and the *yada*-stone immersed in the blood of the cocks. However, it will not lose its power in the first place if it is wrapped into a blue piece of cloth, is kept in a humid place, or is fixed to the tail of a black horse.

The *yada*-ceremony itself takes place on the banks of a river, or in a secluded place. The rain-maker performs an ablution, then he prays to the saints of Islam, and recites the appropriate verses from the Koran. Afterwards, there follows the *yada*-ceremony itself. A black, white, or dappled *yada*-stone is fixed to horse-hair and hung into the river. The prayer continues: the rain-maker addresses the clouds, which he compares

---

[189] *Op. cit.*, p. 154–8. Unfortunately, Malov published only the Russian translations of these texts, and, as Dr. S.G. Klyashtornïy kindly informed me in June 1990, the Eastern Turki originals seem to have been lost from the Malov Fund.

to white and skewbald sheep, and asks them to come over and bring rain.[190] Another version of the *yada*-ceremony[191] is as follows: The *yada*-stone is carefully attached to a single horse-hair and sunk to the bottom of a river. No one but the rain-maker is allowed to see this ceremony. After a while, the soaked stone is taken from the water, and forty-one spoonfuls of the blood of a red cock mixed with water is sprinkled towards the sky, while recitations from the Koran continue. The Aksu manuscript contains the description of another rain-making ceremony: Here, too, the *yada*-stone is fixed to a single horse-hair and sunk into water at a secluded place. Having performed the ritual ablution, the rain-maker goes to the riverside, or to a high place, where he prays and turns forty-one times towards the four quarters of the heavens starting from the West, and then he spits on the ground. If the ceremony is performed this way, clouds appear within an hour, and other miracles can also be seen.[192] A similar rite is described in the Keriya manuscript[193] which does not mention the *yada*-stone as such: Quotations from the Koran are recited, the blood of a red cock is sprinkled towards the sky, the ground surrounding the mosque is spit upon, the participants in the ceremony spend some time sitting in contemplation at a lonely place, and then they sprinkle blood towards the sky and the four cardinal points.

The Aksu manuscript also contains descriptions of rain-making ceremonies attributed in some degree to ethnic groups living in, or near Sinkiang: the "Arabs", the "Kazaks", the "Kirghiz" and the "Tanguts"[194]. However, the "Tangut" *yada*, for example, has an Islamic tinge, as do all the others. The "Kazak" *yada* contains a prayer in which white, grey, and black clouds are spoken of as sheep, or as sheep's heads, or as black *khoja*s. The rain-maker is said to saddle a dappled, a dappled white, a black, and a white horse, and to sacrifice sheep of the same colours. He pitches a white tent and puts on white clothes. There

---

[190] *Op. cit.*, p. 156.

[191] *Op. cit.*, p. 157.

[192] *Op. cit.* p. 158.

[193] *Op. cit.* p. 157.

[194] *I.e.* Tibetan.

are references to a white and lightweight stone submerged in blood.[195] In the "Kirghiz" *yada*-prayer, a big bird with long legs[196] and dappled sheep occur as offerings. The suppliant puts on a black cap, and dresses in black as a sign of mourning. He saddles a black horse to seek favour with the black *khoja*s, that is, the black clouds, and encourages them to ride it, to bring wind and rain. The tiger's head is another metaphor that is used. In the "Tangut" *yada*, the rain-maker puts on black armour and mounts a black horse.[197]

Malov[198] also reports a rite called *yada* which was used by the Uighurs of the Ili River Valley (the Taranchi) to cast a spell over someone. Prayers, called *yada*, are recited over a live frog, and after each prayer, the frog is pricked with a needle. After a few pricks, the frog dies, and is buried under the gate of the person on whom the spell is cast. The person soon grows thin, pale, and dies. Relatives have been known to find the remains of the frog when they searched under the gate of the deceased person's house.[55]

According to Grenard[199], the most powerful and fearful of the magicians is the *ǰadugar,* who can produce abundant crops and can also destroy them, conjure up rain or sunshine, and can cause people to die. To produce rain, the *ǰadugar* takes a jade, a sacred piece of stone in which God's name is engraved and which was given by Noah to Japheth, fixes it to a willow-twig, and submerges it in water.[200]

---

195 *Op. cit.,* p. 159.

196 *I.e.* some kind of water-fowl?

197 *Op. cit.,* p. 160.

198 *Op. cit.,* pp. 153–4.

199 1898, p. 257.

200 Grenard mistook the *yada*-stone for jade here, a common mistake, corrected by Pelliot (1959, pp. 424–5). Furthermore, Grenard confuses *yadačï* 'weather-magician' and *ǰadugar* 'magician'. The *ǰadugar* is a diviner who foretells the future by means of strips of paper on which different prayers, or Cabalistic expressions, are written. The future is told by the *ǰadugar* from the position of the strips of paper, *i.e.* whether they are carried away by the wind, or are carried to the person who wants to see the future (Malov 1918, p. 4). The

Jarring, too, gives a description of rain-makers called *yadačï* in Guma:

> "There are no rain-makers in Guma. There are some in a village called Zonglang, belonging to (the) Qarghaliq(-district). From time immemorial many rain-makers come from this place. As far as I have heard they put the *yada*-stone into water and if they read the prayers (appropriate for) it, it is said that it will rain. If they put the *yada*-stone in a warm place and read the (appropriate) prayers the sun is said to appear. (Now comes) a description of how to find the *yada*-stone. It is believed that the *yada*-stone falls down from Heaven in the autumn. It falls on a lucernefield or in a green field or on such places which are green. If, having got it with grass, an ox eats it. Such an ox, when he is bellowing, will do it to fifteen times and (then) stop. From such an ox some people have found a *yada*-stone. Of course there are people in the Six Cities who have killed such an ox and taken the *yada*-stone... There was a man in Qarghaliq, when he had come to Guma and procured rain once he is said—when he procured rain—to have caused it to rain ice (hail) like green walnuts. The hail hit the heads of some people and their heads are said to have become swollen. It is said to have been in the middle of summer. The hail hit the unripe melons and they are said to have been split (to have gone into pieces). The hail which fell in consequence of the rain-procuring of this man is said to have split the unripe melons of the melon fields. If that man mounted a horse and made the horse gallop he is said to have caused it to rain on the mane of the horse and to snow on its back. When the ice (hail) which this rain-maker had caused to fall hit the beams of the grape-vine

---

ǰadugar is also mentioned briefly by Ol'denburg (1918, p. 20).

> *baraŋ* rattling sounds are said to have come out from the beams. This my father has told me. My mother also knows about these happenings. My father and mother have been sitting telling me about this[201]."

Members of the Swedish Missionary Society also took notice of rain-making around Kashghar, Yengi Hissar and Yarkend:

> If there is a severe drought a rain-maker is called in. Before he begins his task he has, in some solitary place or at a shrine, been reciting no less than 70,000 long prayers during 41 days. The magic performance of rain-making has to be witnessed by the eldest of the people. The magic is performed in the following way. The rain-maker brings a stone which has been found in the intestines of some animal and puts it into a vessel filled with the blood of some quadruped which has recently been slaughtered. This blood is stirred with the help of a whisk made of willow-twigs. Meanwhile the rain-maker recites incantations. The time for the arrival of rain can be indicated, but usually the rain-maker reserves for himself two days of grace. If rain does not appear during this period he asks for a respite of eight days, during which time he prays day and night. If rain does not appear even then it means that the enemies of the rain-maker are working against him. They are able to prevent the rain through counteracting incantations. The rain-makers make people pay well for their services. But if they fail completely it happens that they receive a well deserved punishment by the people who feel deceived. The same may happen if they procure too much rain. There are

---

[201] Jarring 1946–1951, iv, pp. 168–70.

> also wind-makers but they are not as important as rain-makers.
>
> If there is no rain people go to the rain-makers, bringing them generous offerings, sometimes several *yambo* [*i.e.* a lump of silver], in order to have them procure rain. If the rain thus procured becomes too heavy it happens that people drag the rain-maker to the Chinese court. The mandarins then sentence him to a couple of hundreds whiplashes and put him in the stocks for a couple of weeks. Some years ago two rain-makers were thus punished by the *Shen-guan* [*i. e.* by the chief of district].[202]

The Yellow Uighurs present a special case, living as they do mixed with the Mongolian-speaking Shera Yögurs, and surrounded by the Chinese and the Tibetans, and thus isolated from other Turkic peoples. Potanin[203] provides some rather fragmentary pieces of information on the weather-magic of the Yellow Uighurs. A round loaf is made of drugs and spices and a bucketful of water is fetched from a nearby spring. The loaf is plunged into the water, and a *nom* 'prayer' is said over it. When it begins to rain, the water is taken and poured back into the spring from which it was taken. The ritual is called *ǰadalana* 'doing weather-magic'.

The Turkic Peoples of Siberia

In Siberia, *d'ada* is common among the Southern tribes of the Altai Turks. The Altai Turkic *d'adačï*'s function differs from that of the *kam*, his job being to control the weather by means of the *d'ada-taš* that can be found on rocks exposed to constant wind. To obtain the magic stone, the weather-magician will sacrifice all his fortune and sell all his livestock.

---

[202] Jarring 1979—80, pp. 13—4.

[203] 1893, i, p. 442.

He is, thus, sometimes reduced to utter poverty, with no wife or children. To produce clear weather, the stone must be placed in a dry and hot place, or under the deltoid muscle. To produce wind, it must be exposed to the fresh air. If a cold northerly wind is needed, for example, to keep a horse from sweating on a hot day, the *d'ada-taš* is fixed to the horse's mane. To produce bad weather, it is placed into cold water for a day or so.[204] The Telengits, one of the Southern Altaian Turkic tribes, find the *d'ada-taš* in the taiga. They believe that if it is accidentally dropped into a river, it will snow for forty days and nights. Any fire can be extinguished by means of the stone; it must, therefore, be handled carefully. It is used in hunting to produce the kind of snow in which wounded wolves will leave a trail. According to local beliefs in the Ust'-Kanskiy rayon of the Altai Mountains, there is a cave in which the rain-stone can be found. If children happen to go into this cave, and accidentally break the *d'ada-taš* into pieces, it will begin to snow or rain, depending on the season of the year. Other objects are also used among the Southern Altai Turkic tribes to change the weather, for instance the healed paws of animals wounded by hunters, healed when the animal ate some magic herb. When the wounded game is finally killed, the healed paw is cut off and kept to use as a *d'ada* to produce rain or snow in case of need.[205] On the other hand, Potapov[206] reports that the Teleut clan of the Altai Turks does not know the rain-stone, and pray to the Rain-God Totoi-Padian to bring rain.

Another kind of weather magic is recounted in the epic tale *Kān Püdäi* without the *d'ada* being mentioned. The hero, Kara Attū kān's son, who was given the name Kān Püdäi, when trailing seven wolves, works weather-magic using his horse to be able to follow the tracks of the seven wolves:

Jetzt stieg der Jüngling auf,

---

[204] Verbitskiy 1893, p. 45.

[205] Alekseev 1980, pp. 47–8.

[206] 1978, p. 18.

Laut pfiff er,
Heftig schrie er,
Neun Spannen Schnee fielen,
Ein heisser schwarzer Wind kam,
Der Jüngling folgte der Spur der sieben Wölfe,
Sechs Berggipfel Überschritt er,
Diesseits des siebenten Berggipfels
Lagen die sieben Wölfe im Schnee.[207]

In an Altai Turkic tale, the horse named Temchi-eren belonging to the hero Altay Buchïy does weather-magic (*d'ada*) with his mane and tail, and it snows till the snow is as high as the horse's head.[208]

The Khakass tribes, living east of the Altai Turks, are unfamiliar with the rain-stone. The shamans of the Saghais, one of the Khakass tribes, draw clouds on their drums. Members of the other Khakass tribe, the Kachas, ask the mountains for rainfall[209], and they believe that rain can be produced by spilling bear's gall over the ground.[210]

In 1861, Radloff[211] witnessed a weather-making ceremony on his journey to Siberia which he describes as follows:

> Während unseres Aufenthaltes am Kara Köl hatten wir meist trockenes Wetter, so dass sich unsere Pferde, deren Hufe von den steinigen Wegen und vom Regen sehr angegriffen waren, ziemlich erholt hatten.
>
> Leider begann schon gestern wieder das gewöhnliche schlechte Wetter und unsere Führer

---

[207] Altaian text: Radloff 1866, i, pp. 64–5, German translation ii, p. 67.

[208] Nikiforov 1915, p. 14.

[209] Potapov, *op. cit.*

[210] Alekseev 1980, p. 50.

[211] 1893, ii, pp. 179–80.

> beschlossen, da wir heute abreisen wollten, einen Versuch zu machen, gutes Wetter herbei zu zaubern.
>
> Der Glaube an das Bannen der Witterung ist bei allen Völkern des Altai sowie auch bei Sojonen verbreitet. Es giebt gewisse Familien, in denen sich diese Kraft von dem Vater auf den Sohn vererbt. Einige dieser Wetterzwinger sind weit und breit berühmt und man sagt, dass es Menschen giebt, die das Wetter so beherrschen, dass sie machen können, dass die Sonne dir in's Gesicht scheint und zugleich der Regen den Rücken durchnässt. Zum Besprechen des Wetters bedient man sich eines Wettersteines (jada tasch), der vor mir angewandte war ein Bergkrystall. Dieser Stein muss aber gewisse Eigenschaften haben, an denen ihn nur der Eingeweihte zu erkennen vermag, die aber, da sie ein Geheimniss sind, mir nicht mitgetheilt wurden.
>
> Eine Sojonenfrau brachte einen Jada-tasch herbei und einer meiner Führer führte mit diesem die Ceremonie aus. Er befestigte den Stein zuerst über's Feuer und liess ihn vom Rauche beschlagen, dann schwang er den Stab nach allen Seiten in der Luft umher, während er mit lauter Stimme die Beschwörungsformel sang.

The ritual was performed in the territory of Tuva by means of a piece of stone—actually a rock-crystal—provided by a local Tuva woman, but the weather-magic was done by Radloff's guide who himself belonged to the Tölös tribe of the Altai Turks. The ritual, thus, had some kind of South Siberian "inter-tribal" character. The text of the incantation was given by Radloff elsewhere as follows:

> Kairakan! Kairakan!
> Alas! Alas! Alas!
> Wie eine Handfläche gross mach' eine Oeffnung!

Wie eine Nadel gross mache ein Loch!
Ich, der Same vom Geschlecht (d. h. der
Regenmacher),
Die Wurzel des Cedernbaumes,
Abu Toby hat gerufen,
Ongostoi Kuldurak hat gerufen,
Der Nabel des Himmels möge an der Erde sein!
Der Nabel der Erde möge im Himmel sein!
Den Ahnherrn Paschtygasch rufe ich an,
Den Weg des Himmels öffne!
Wie eine Handfläche gross mache eine Oeffnung!
Wie eine Nadel gross mache ein Loch!
Von der Hinterseite der hohen Berge aus dringe
hindurch!
Von der Abakan-Quelle aus dringe hindurch!
Kairakan! Kairakan!
Alas! Alas! Alas![212]

The Tuvins of the Mongun-taiga and of Kara-khol believe that the weather can be influenced with the *čat taš*, and with certain plants. The *čat taš* is a piece of white, red or black stone which the Tuvins of Kara-khol believe can be found along the upper reaches of the Chulchi River, near the Üttüg-khol Lake, and among the rocks of the mountains of Uch Kïrlu Kaya, or Sodon Kaya. To produce rain, the *čat taš* must be put into a river and sprinkled with water from above. If the stone is kept in the river long enough to grow cold, there will be much snow. If it is left in the river permanently, the river will dry up. The story was told in the Mongun-taiga of a translucent white *čat taš* on a peak near the Kargï

---

[212] Altai Turkic text 1866, i, pp. 220–1, German translation ii, pp. 241–2.

River. Clouds could be seen in the stone, as in a mirror, if someone gazed into it attentively. To bring on rain, one needed to place it in a river.[213] The Todjin clan of the Tuvas believe that rain-stones in the shape of a human figure are to be found in the crops of wood-grouse and in the intestines of some other animals. The Todjins keep the stone wrapped in cloth, and use it to procure snow for the hunt.[214]

The Yakuts believe that the *sata* 'magic stone' can be found very early in the morning under trees struck by lightning. One must look for it at dawn, because the *sata* dies in the sun. The *sata* can also be acquired from the intestines of horses, bulls, bears, wolves, dogs, ducks, geese, eagles and other animals. The most powerful *sata*s are those found in wolves; they can produce drought and strong winds. All *sata*s can cause wind, cold and snow in high summer. The *sata* resembles a man's head, but is smaller. If it is touched by a woman, or is seen by foreigners, it dies. If thrown into hot water, it goes round and round, giving off a hissing sound in the pot, till it grows still and dies. The dead *sata* is like an ordinary piece of stone.

When a living *sata* held in the palm is lifted towards the sky, a cold wind begins to blow immediately. If someone who owns a *sata* sets out on a journey, he will fix the stone under the mane or tail of his horse; the horse will not sweat, and a cold breeze will keep off the mosquitoes. To keep its power, the *sata* needs to be wrapped in the hide of the animal in whose body it was found, and kept in the hollow of a tree. Once a *sata*-stone resembling a man's head was found in the droppings of an eagle. If the stone was turned towards the sun and thrown upwards, then tapped once, the wind blew the following day. If it was tapped two or three times, the wind blew the following two or three days.[215]

---

[213] Potapov 1960, p. 236.

[214] Alekseev 1980, pp. 56–7. For Potanin's (1883, pp. 189–90) discussion of this belief among the Uriankhais (Tuvins), see below.

[215] Seroshevskiy 1896, pp. 668–9; [Sieroszewski] 1902, pp. 214–5.

The Yakuts living in the district of Vilyuy believed the *sata* to be a translucent gray, of a form reminiscent of the human body. It develops in human calves. It grows there slowly over thirty or forty years, causing strong pain as it moves around in the calf. Finally, a small wound appears under the knee, and the *sata*-stone emerges through this wound. Sometimes the stone has "children": smaller stones that appear any time between four to forty days following its appearance. The *sata*-stone must be kept hidden in a leather bag by its owner, and can be taken out only in case of necessity. To influence the weather, the Yakuts of Vilyuy slowly immerse the *sata*-stone in water three times, holding it with their thumb and forefinger, cursing themselves and all their future descendants all the while: "May neither I myself, nor any of my descendants see any good come from the gods, or from any human being, but only from you, *sata*! May rain pour—or may it snow—for x number of days!"[216]

The Yakuts of Verkhoyansk believed in the existence of different kinds of *sata*. One of them was the *eting satata*, the 'thunderbolt-*sata*' that can be found at sunrise between the roots of trees struck by lightning. Besides weather-magic, the *sata*-stone is used by the Yakuts of Verkhoyansk also for other purposes. *Sata* found in the hearts of mares is good for protecting new-born babies if swung around the cradle, but it also cures the diseases of livestock if carried around in their pen. No shaman's curse will have any effect on the possessor of this kind of *sata*. Still another *sata* in Verkhoyansk is the eagle-*sata* which resembles a duck's egg. It brings luck to its owner in all his efforts, and is, therefore, sometimes called *d'ol taaha*, 'stone of luck'. Its owner becomes a favourite of fortune, as long as he keeps it on himself wrapped in a piece of fur all the time. After five or six years, one should pull it out from the fur, smear the stone with butter and wrap it again. Should the owner of the eagle-*sata* want to drive mosquitoes and gadflies off his cattle, he fixes the *sata* to a birch-rod, and carries it around the cattle, saying: *Op-čuk! op-čuk! Arčï! ǰay böγö ǰalbarïydïn, kölǰün böγö kötöγöhünnün!*

---

[216] Popov 1949, p. 288.

"Op-čuk! op-čuk! Arčï![217] Let the evil spirit go away, let the insect disappear!" One can also foresee the future with the help of the eagle-*sata*. Its owner hangs it on a pole: if an easterly wind begins to blow immediately, it means good luck; if a northerly, the owner of the *sata* will have luck with his cows. If a southerly wind rises, an important person can be expected to arrive; a westerly wind, however, means impending death: that of the owner, of his children, or of his wife. The Yakuts of Verkhoyansk are also reported to use square crystals, and black, flat stones as *sata*, the latter resembling a human face without eyebrows and beard. Some owners keep the *sata*-stones in three-ply boxes wrapped in hare's fur, others hide the *sata* in their clothes, somewhere near their left shoulder, or sew them into the upper part of their caps.[218]

The Buriats

According to the beliefs of the Buriats of Balagan, the twentieth of the fifty-three gods occupying the Western Sky is *Zada Sagan Tengeri*[219] who commands the *zada*-wind that brings rain or snow, a wind that does not blow for long, but rises several times a day. The *zada*-wind occurs mostly in the autumn and the spring. The *zada*, *i.e.* bad weather, can be brought on with the help of a certain root which, if wrenched or dug out from under the ground, produces thorough change of weather: it cools down rapidly, a strong wind rises and brings rain or snow over a period of three, five, seven or nine days. Hunters in the taiga know this root

[217] *Arčï* is an exclamatory word, used when the Yakut perambulate their yurt, carrying a piece of burning wood, and say prayers to exorcise the evil spirits which cause illness (Pekarskiy 1917, c. 153).

[218] Khudyakov 1969, p. 277.

[219] 'Zada White God'; sometimes he is called Zada Ulan Tengeri 'Zada Red God' (Khangalov 1890, p. 6, n. 3), the fifty-third *tengeri* in the Western Sky, who precipitates red *zada*-stones from the sky (*op. cit.*, p. 10).

very well, and make the *zada* assist them in their hunts. The root is also known to the big birds, like geese and swans which make *šubuni zada,* 'bird-*zada*'[220] to help them in their southward migration in the autumn. Some quadrupeds, like the deer and the elk, also know this root; then it is called *bugan zada*, 'deer-*zada*'.[221]

A certain red stone, the *Zadan Ulan Sulun*[222] is also mentioned in connection with the *zada*: it, too, can bring on the *zada*-wind. Sometimes, *zada* comes on when a fulgurite falls into water. In this case, it lasts for nine days. *Zada* 'bad weather' must, in any case, be distinguished from ordinary rain, snow or wind.[223]

The Western Mongols

The belief that weather can be influenced is widespread among the Western Mongols. Potanin[224] reports that throughout Northern Mongolia, there is a common belief in a stone which can produce rain. It is called *dzada* by the Dörböts, and *džada* by the Uriankhais and the Altai Turks.[225] Some people say that it occurs in the mountains; others claim that it can be obtained from snakes' heads. The Dörböts think that the Uriankhais possess such stones; that is why the weather is always bad when the Uriankhais come to plunder the land of the Dörböts. One can find the *dzada*-stone in the heads of beasts such as deer, or in those of

---

[220] See Buriat *šubuu(n)* 'a bird' (Cheremisov 1973, p. 731).

[221] See Buriat *buga* 'a deer, maral' (*op. cit.*, p. 108).

[222] See Buriat *ulaan* 'red', and *šuluu(n)* 'stone' (*op. cit.*, pp. 466 and 733).

[223] Khangalov 1890, p. 6.

[224] 1883, pp. 189—90, 773—4.

[225] Potanin is not very specific on the linguistic forms here. *džada* can only be Mongolian Uriankhai, because according to other sources (see above), the forms *čat*, and *d'ada* can be expected as the Turkic Uriankhai (Tuvinian) and the Altaian forms respectively.

birds, such as ducks. *Dzada*-stones are found also in the stomachs of bulls. These are black and streaky, and are in the size of a fist. Some frauds will claim ordinary pieces of stones to be *dzada*-stones. So as not to be cheated, one must learn to recognize a real *dzada*-stone: it is so cold that one can hardly bear to hold it, and put to one's ear, it gives a crackling sound. When bad weather is needed, the stone is soaked in some water that is in its natural state: cups and man-made holes, for instance, are unsuitable. The stone must also be sprinkled with water in the sun. The stone is active for three years; then it dies. However, it can be revitalized. For this purpose, an animal of the same kind as the one from which the *dzada*-stone was taken must be wounded by a shot, and the *dzada*-stone must be placed under the breath of the dying quadruped or bird. The death of the *dzada* can be prevented by wrapping it in the feathers of the kind of bird, or the hide of the kind of animal from which it had been taken. If the *dzada* is too effective, *i.e.* there is too much rain, the *dzada*-stone is dried out.

The belief in the *dzada*-stone is so strong in Northern Mongolia that all kinds of bad weather are attributed to it. If it is cold, it is taken to mean that someone is making the *dzada*-stone work to freeze the river because he wants to cross it. If it snows, it is assumed that the Uriankhais have done weather-magic because they want to follow the tracks of some game. Certain roots are also used to bring on bad weather.

According to the eighteenth century Manchu author, Ch'i-shi-yi, the Torgut and Ölöt tribes of the Oirats of Turkestan, when they set off on a long journey in the summer, often fix a bezoar in a small bag to their horses' tails to provide some cool breeze on the journey.[226] In the Sinkiang version of the Oirat *J̌anγar* epic, one of the omens of the hero's future career is the fact that he is born firmly holding a piece of blue *zada*-stone in his left hand.[227]

---

[226] Iakinf 1829, p. 214.

[227] Kičikov 1985, pp. 351–2.

The weather-magic practiced by the Kalmucks living by the Volga River in the eighteenth century has been described by Pallas:[228]

> Unter die von der Lamaischen Geistlichkeit gebilligten und ausgeübten Zaubereyen gehört zuförderst das Wettermachen (*Sadda-Barinä*). Nicht nur geringe Geistliche, sondern auch Schriftkundige unter den gemeinen oder schwarzen Kalmücken geben sich damit ab. Sie rühmen sich nicht nur das Wetter auf einige Tage vorher bestimmen, sondern auch, bey obwaltender Dürre, über eine ganze Gegend Regen bringen zu können, am heitern Himmel eine Wolke zu schaffen, bey großer Hitze eine kühle Luft, bey stillem Wetter, Wind und bey klarer Luft Nebel erregen zu können. Sie wollen auch im Stande seyn aufsteigende Wolken zu vertreiben, wenn sie durch ähnliche menschliche Zaubereyen entstanden sind; welches sie daran erkennen wollen, wenn solche Wolken zuerst, als ganz kleines Gewölk, am Horizont aufsteigen. — Die Wetterzauberey beruhet auf gewissen Formeln der geheimnißvollen Sprache (*Tarni*)[229] welche mit gläubigem Herzen und tiefer Andacht von dem Wettermacher (*Saadutschi*) gegen gewisse Götzen hergemurmelt werden. Um Regen zu verschaffen muß die Andacht zum Beyspiel an den Götzen *Otschirbani* gerichtet werden, und die Formel ist: *Um chum sungni nagarasa gangpük ßoocha!* Damit Wolken aufsteigen, hilft folgendes an *Mansuschiri* Burchan gerichtetes Gebet: *Um ssarwa gharma karem laalik ßoocha!* Nebel erweckt eine an den Burchan

[228] 1776–1801, ii, pp. 348–50.

[229] See Mong. *tarni* '[Sanskrit *dhāraṇī*] Magic spell mostly consisting of Sanskrit syllables or words and/or unintelligeble phonetic units used in religious and quasi-religious rites charms, dharani, mantra.' (Lessing 1960, p. 781).

Nagansana gerichtete Formel: *Um zartschu ningwo riih rewok!* Kühle Luft giebt der Burchan *Radnasambowa*, auf folgende Beschwörungsworte: *Um naga jöh jagi ssoocha!* Um Regenwolken zu vertreiben wendet man sich an die obgenannten vier Burchanen und *Chonschin boddi ssado*, mit der Formel: *Um jadda nagara tschiltschil polpol ßoocha!* Auch um Sturmwind zu verursachen wird zum Götzen *Chondschin hoddissado* gebetet und zwar mit folgender Formul: *Um ghom dam pat püngh ssocha!*

Solche *Tarni* werden kniend gebetet, und z. E. um Regen zu machen, in eine Schale voll Wasser, nach geendigtem Gebet, gewisse Steinchen gethan, die man mit dem Wasser, nach der Himmelsgegend, woher der Regen kommen soll, ausschüttet. Um Sturm zu erregen wird nur Staub oder Sand nach den Beschwörungen ausgeschüttet. Sie erzählen auch viel von einem Steinchen (*Saadan Tscholon*), welches zuweilen auf der Erde oder auch in Thiermägen gefunden wird und sich im Wasser beständig im Wirbel bewegen soll, so daß das Wasser in der Schale gleichsam in eine kochende Bewegung geräth. Werden dabey die gehörigen *Tarni* ausgesprochen, so erfolgt ohnfehlbar Platzregen.

Wer die Kunst des Wettermachens ausüben will, der muß wie die Kalmücken sagen, festen Glauben an der Macht obgedachter Götzen, welche dieser *Tarni* Erfinder sind, fassen, und in diesem Glauben einmahl in seinem Leben die zu gebrauchende Formuln, jede Einhunderttausendmahl hinter einander andächtig hergesagt haben. Will er nachmals Gebrauch davon machen, so muß er die erforderte Formul, es sey, nach den Umständen, stehend, sitzend oder knieend, voll Andacht und festen Glauben, fünfhundertmahl hersagen, und würkt diese Portion nicht, noch fünfhundertmahl, welches denn nie fehlschlagen soll. Ja die Kalmücken versichern, daß auch

> Russen, denen die Kunst recht gelernt worden und die sie mit rechtem Glauben ausüben, dieselbe Kraft, Wetter zu machen, besitzen. Es sind aber zwey Ausnahmen zu bemerken: erstlich so darf die Kunst nicht im Winter ausgeübt werden, weil sie Gewächsen und Thieren schädlich werden könnte und also sündlich ist, zweytens, so ist es auch im Sommer Sünde gar zu oft Regen und Ungewitter zu zaubern, weil vieles Gewürm und Ungeziefer dadurch umkommt.

According to Bergmann[230], who travelled among the Kalmucks in 1802—03, the weather-magicians[231] allegedly had command over rain, sunshine, thunder and lightning, and were often consulted in all these matters. In the summer, they used bezoar stones which, for some natural reasons, emitted some kind of vapour when put in water. The vapour produced this way was considered to be the core from which the clouds developed. The *Ssaddatschi* tended to produce this vapour particularly when it already looked like rain. A weather-magician disappointed in his hopes, could explain his failure by saying that another *Ssaddatschi* was working against him, or that the heat was too strong to be overcome by rain. Finally, a *Ssaddatschi* called on to do weather-magic at a time when rain was unlikely, would decline to cooperate, saying that the rain-magic would be harmful to the insects.

---

230 1804, iii, pp. 183—4.

231 *Ssaddatschi*, the weather-magician, is one, of two kinds of Kalmuck sorcerers mentioned by Bergmann (*op. cit.*, iii, pp. 183—4). The other is the *Dallatschi*, who can foretell the weather by reading the *Dalla* 'sheep's, swine's, or deer's shoulderblade'. The shoulderblade was burned in fire; if the flames left large smuts on the bone, a mild winter could be expected; if it stayed rather white, the winter would be cold with much snow.

THE MONGUORS

Potanin[232] also recounts a rain-making ceremony performed by the Monguors[233] of San-Ch'uan. The ceremony took place in a Buddhist shrine[234] situated on the Yellow River, built in a cave in which there were several springs. Water dripping from the rock-walls of the cave accumulated in a basin. In case of drought, the people, led by the heads of the local community, proceeded to the cave carrying images of the Chinese god Lung Wang, "The Dragon King", and placed them next to the springs in the cave. The ceremony shows the influence of Chinese popular beliefs and rites on the Monguors as well as the influence of Buddhism.

THE ORDOS MONGOLS

Rain-making among the Ordos Mongols of Inner Mongolia in the twentieth century has been described by Mostaert[235]. At times of draught, the Ordos Mongols invoke rain with the help of the rain-stone (*DžaDa*), a round white stone the size of a pheasant's egg. The lamas, asked by the community to "invite" the rain, proceed to a marshy spot. Here they dig down until they reach water. Having previously poured a little water into an earthenware jar, they put the rain-stone into it and place the jar in the little well they have dug, so that the bottom of the jar is in the water. Then, the lamas begin their prayers which go on for three days and sometimes longer. During that time, those who had invited the lamas could neither smoke, nor drink spirits, nor eat meat. It is unclear

---

232 1893, i, p. 377.

233 In Potanin's terminology "Shirongol".

234 *Op. cit.*, pp. 337–8.

235 1956, pp. 291–2.

from Mostaert's account what kind of "stone" the *DžaDa* of the Ordos is, but it is, presumably, some kind of bezoar. For we know from Potanin's description[236] that there are two sorts of *džada* 'rain-stone' among the Ordos: the snake-*džada* (*mogoin džada*), and the donkey-*džada* (*eldžigen džada*). The first is located at the bifurcation of the tail of fork-tailed snakes, the other kind of *džada* can be found in the dung of black donkeys (*xara eldžigen*). The latter is particularly effective. The *džada*-stone produces rain if it is kept under spring water.

A rain-making ceremony of another kind from the Ordos is reported by Mostaert[237]: the lamas perform a ceremony and recite the *yöm* in a temple, on a hill, or by a spring in order to bring on rain.

---

236 1893, ii, p. 352. Potanin's informant was "a Mongol from the Ordos, named Punsuk".

237 1968, p. 404, under *yöm*.

THE LINGUISTIC ARGUMENT

The Turkic and Mongolian words for 'weather-magic' have so far been quoted as found in the sources—transcribed, if written in other scripts—but they have not been analyzed linguistically. What now follows, therefore, is such an analysis, since the linguistic argument provides important evidence for the history of weather-magic in Inner Asia. Though on the face of it there are a great variety of words meaning 'weather-magic' in the Turkic and Mongolian languages, as a matter of fact—apart from a few terms like Ott. *yağmur duası* 'a prayer for rain' or Chuv. *śumăr čükĕ* 'id.' which do not require detailed linguistic analysis—there is, etymologically speaking, a homogeneity behind the various forms of Tu. *yay*, *ǰay*, *yada*, *sata*, Mo. *ǰada*, etc. All these words belong together, and, in one way or other, come from an Old Turkic word attested in the Old Turkic sources as *yād* or *yāt*. One can only agree with Clauson[238] that OTu. *yād* has an extremely complicated history, and both anthropological and linguistic studies abound in imprecise, and sometimes erroneous forms and meanings for the several variants of the word. Its history deserves special attention.

Tu. *yada* and *ǰada* first became known to European scholarship through Chaghatai texts, and Vámbéry[239] was the first to discuss their etymology. He thought to detect in the word a trace of the impact of Zoroastrian civilization on the Turks, and compared Tu. *yada* and *ǰada* to OIr. *yātu* and Pe. *ǰādū* 'magic'. Similarly, Munkácsi[240] included Tu. *yada* and *ǰadu* in his list of Aryan loan-words in Turkic. The Iranian origin of Tu. *yada* is now widely accepted, though the date of the borrowing and the identity of the lending Iranian language has not been clari-

---

238 1972, p. 883.

239 1879, pp. 249—50 and 1885, p. 54.

240 1900, p. 157.

fied. Some[241] speak of an unspecified "Old Iranian borrowing", others[242] compare the Turkic forms to Pe. *jādū*. Explaining the Mongolian form, Ramstedt[243] and Poppe[244] have suggested that Mo. *ǰada* was a loan from Turkic, which itself had been a borrowing of Pe. *jadū*. This view has been rejected by Clauson[245]. Finally, Doerfer[246] established that the word under discussion had two variants in Turkic: the monosyllabic forms developed from OTu. *yād*, and the disyllabic *yada* or *ǰada*, both of which are borrowings from Mongolian. Consequently, the disyllabic forms cannot be compared to any Iranian word.

First of all, it may be useful to reiterate once more that Mo. *ǰada* and Tu. *ǰada* or *yada* 'weather-magic' are not to be confused with NPe. *jādū*, which means 'magic' and not 'weather-magic' in the narrower sense. NPe. *jādū* 'conjuration, magic' and its derivative *jādūgar* 'a juggler, a conjurer'[247] have been borrowed by several Turkic languages beginning with Middle Turkic: *ǰadï* 'Sihirbaz, büyücü'[248]; and it also can be found in the following New Turkic languages: Oghuz: Ott. *jādū* (vulg. *jadı*) 'A wizard, a witch; Witchcraft, sorcery; a spell', *jādūger* 'A witch, a sorcerer'[249], Az. *ǰadu* 'magiya, charï, koldovstvo', *ǰadukär* 'volshebnik, zaklinatel', koldun, etc.'[250], Gag. *ǰadï* 'koldun, koldun'ya'[251], Trkm. *ǰa:dï* 'koldovstvo, volshebstvo, etc.', *ǰa:dïgöy*

---

[241] Brockelmann 1925, p. 112; Harva 1938, pp. 221—23; Malov 1947, p. 154; Schmidt 1949, pp. 67 and 270; Räsänen 1969, pp. 122 and 176—7 and Aalto 1971, p. 31. None of these authors go beyond Vámbéry's and Munkácsi's works.

[242] Marquart 1914, p. 37, note 5; Ramstedt 1935, p. 462; 1952, p. 9.

[243] *Op. cit.*

[244] 1955a, p. 39.

[245] *Op. cit.*

[246] 1963—75, i, pp. 286—9; iv, p. 142.

[247] Steingass 1892, p. 349.

[248] Izbudak 1936, p. 8.

[249] Redhouse 1890, p. 634.

[250] *AzRS 1965*, p. 400.

[251] *GagMRS 1973*, p. 183.

'koldun, volshebnik, etc.'[252]; Kipchak: CrimT. *ǰadu, ǰadu qarï* 'die Hexe'[253], Kar. *džadu* 'koldun, charodey', *džaduv* 'koldun, koldun'ya, ved'ma', *džaduvluχ, džaduluk* 'koldovstvo'[254], Kirgh. *ǰadï, ǰadu ir.* 'magiya, volshebstvo, charodeystvo', *ǰadïger, ǰadïgöy, ǰadugöy* 'zaklinatel', mag, charodey'[255], Kaz. *ǰadu* 'witch-craft, sorcery', *ǰadï* 'sorcerer', *ǰadïyar* 'foreteller'[256]; Eastern: Uzb. *ǰodu* 'koldovstvo, volshebstvo, etc.', *ǰodugar* 'koldun, volshebnik, etc.'[257], ETurki *ǰadu* p. 'koldovstvo, zaklinanie, etc.', *ǰadigär* 'koldun, volshebnik, etc.'[258]. So, this word cannot directly be connected with either *ǰada* or *yada*. Mo. *ǰadu* referred to by Poppe[259] got into the Mongolian part of the *Muqaddimat al-Adab* from Persian through Turkic mediation.

The Turkic words for 'weather-magic', as has been pointed out above, are either mono- or disyllabic. The monosyllabic forms are attested since the Old Turkic period: Old Turkic: Uigh. *yad* in *yad yadla-* 'to perform magic'[260], *yatčï* 'Zauberer'[261], *yad yadla-* 'to perform weather-magic', *yadčï är* 'weather-magician', *yad tašï* 'rain-stone'[262], *yad tašlarï* 'rain-stones'[263], Kashgh. *yāt*, *yat* 'a type of divination (*kahāna*) using special stones with which one brings on rain, wind, etc.'[264] *yātčï* '(*kāhin*) diviner' *yatla-* '(*takahhana*) to divine' *yatlat-* '(*yatakahhana*) to order someone to divine[265]; Middle Turkic: Chagh. *yāy* '(1) (*kamān*) bow (2) (*faṣl-i tābistān*) summer (3) (*'ilm-i yada ... 'ilm-i yā mī-nāmand ba-sabab-i īnke bīštar-i ikhtiyāj ba-ān 'amal dar*

---

252 *TrkmRS 1968*, p. 317.
253 Radloff 1888–1911, iv, c. 47.
254 *KarRPS 1974*, p. 171.
255 Yudakhin 1965 pp. 210, 211.
256 Shnitnikov 1966, p. 87.
257 Borovkov 1959, p. 157.
258 Nadzhip 1968, p. 358.
259 *Op. cit.*
260 Gabain 1958, pp. 28–29, 36, 38 reads *yat yatla-*.
261 Müller 1910, p. 84.
262 MIK III 192.
263 T II S [U 3004].
264 Dankoff–Kelly 1982–85, ii, pp. 514, 445.
265 *Op. cit*, ii, p. 307.

tābistān 'ittifāq mīy-uftād) the same as *'ilm-i yada* [that is also] called *'ilm-i yā*, because the principal need for such a practice arises in the summer'[266] *yayčī* '(*kamāngar bāshad, va jādūgar ham gūyand*) bow-maker and magician'[267], Kangli *yay* '(*'ilm-i yāy, ya 'nī isti 'māl-i ḥajar al-maṭar*) the art of *yāy*, that is the use of the rain-stone'[268]; New Turkic: Kipchak: Bashk. *yäy* 'weather-magic'[269], TobolT *yäyši* '(the same as *yadačī*) koldun (sobstv. zogovarivayushchiy dozhd')' *yäyši χatun* 'koldun'ya' *yäyšilik* 'koldovstvo' *yäyšilämäk* 'koldovat', zagovarivat', vorozhit''[270], *yaycï* 'the same as *yaičī*, ein Zauberer, Hexenmeister' *yaicï katïn* 'eine Hexe' *yaicïla-* 'hexen' *yaicïlïq* 'die Zauberei'. Relying on Uighur and Khakani data, **yād* can be reconstructed in Old Turkic. In Khakani, **yād* developed into *yāt*; otherwise, the OTu. *yād* › *yāδ* › MTu. *yay* sound change took place. In the case of the Chagh. *yāy*, the *alif* denotes /ā/. Besides that given in the *Sanglakh*, the only Middle Turkic form appears in Juvaini's work in connection with the weather-magic performed by a Kangli magician in Mongol service. Evidently, the word is not Mongolian, but Turkic, and it may be a specifically Kangli form. Not much is known about the language of the Kangli, but since they are mentioned in the sources in connection with the Kipchaks, in the case of Juvaini's *yay* a Middle Kipchak form can be assumed. The regular developments of OTu. *yād* survived in the NTu. Kipchak languages and in Tuvinian (see *Map 2*).

As a consequence of the Middle Turkic **yād* › *yay* sound change, there occurred a homophonic clash with Tu. *yay* 'summer'[271]. The author of the *Sanglakh*, Muḥammad Mahdī Khān "explains" that the art of *yada* is also called the art of *yā* (‹ *yāy*), "because the principal need for this practice is in the summer". The same popular etymology can be found also in Bashkir. In Chaghatai *yāy* (‹ OTu. *yād*) became homophonic

266 *Sanglakh* 340v. 26–29.

267 *Sanglakh* 341r. 5.

268 Qazvīnī 1912, p. 152.

269 Oral communication by J. Torma.

270 Budagov 1869–71, ii, p. 346.

271 Clauson 1972, p. 980.

with *yāy* 'bow' (‹ OTu. *yā*), thus in the *Sanglakh yāyčï* means both 'bow-maker (*kamāngar*)' and 'weather-magician (*jādūgar*)'.[272]

Mo. *ǰada* is a loan from an OTu. *ǰ*-dialect, and it belongs to the second layer of Turkic loan-words in Mongolian.[273] The Turkic form must have been **ǰādǎ*. The earliest occurrence of Mo. *ǰada* is in the *Secret History*, and it is common in the New Mongolian languages: Middle Mongolian: *jada* 'Regensturm, etwas, was Regen herbeiführen kann, Regenzauber'[274], LMo. *ǰada* 'un temps pluvieux' *ǰada bariqu* 'faire mauvais temps par la magie' *ǰada čilaγun* 'pierre (yada-tache, bézoar) qui fait le mauvais temps' *ǰadači* 'un magicien qui change le temps'[275]; New Mongolian: Bur. *zada* 'nenast'e, nepogoda'[276], Kh. *zad* 'nenast'e, nepogoda'[277], Oir. *dzadǎ* (Dörböt, Dzhakhachin, Bayit, Khoton dialects); *zadǎ* (Dörböt, Dzhakhachin, Ölöt, Torghut dialects) 'zad; nenast'e, nepogoda'[278], Kalm. *zad* '1) der Bezoar, der Regenstein (mit dem man angeblich Regen hervorrufen kann | *z. tšolūn* id.; 2) Niederschlag jeder Art, Regen | *z. tatx* Regen herbeiziehen; *zadīn ūlṇ̥* Regenwolke; *zadin nom* Gebet um Regen. [*ǰada*, *ǰadu*, čag. alt. osm. *jada*; ‹ p. afgh. *ǰādū* 'magisch']'[279], Ordos *DžaDa* 'pierre à pluie' | *DžaDāē tš'ilū* 'id.'; *DžaDāē lama* 'lama qui au moyen d'une pierre à pluie peut faire pleuvoir'; *DžaDa 'tš'i* dans *DžaDa 'tš'i lama* 'lama qui sait faire tomber la pluie au moyen d'une pierre à pluie'[280], Üjümchin *DžäD* (Üǰümčin de l'Ouest, abaga) 'intempérie'[281].

---

[272] Radloff (1888–1911, iii, c. 14) wrongly explains *yayči* as 'der Zauberer, Wahrsager (gewiss ursprünglich mit Hülfe eines Bogens' similarly confounding *yay* 'weather-magic' and *yay* 'a bow', corrected by Doerfer, *op. cit.* p. 288.

[273] Clauson 1962, pp. 220–21.

[274] *SHM*, p. 84.

[275] Kowalewski 1844–49, iii, pp. 2277–8.

[276] Cheremisov 1973, p. 243.

[277] Luvsandéndév 1957, p. 187.

[278] Tsoloo 1988, p. 230.

[279] Ramstedt 1935, p. 462.

[280] Mostaert 1968, i, pp. 177a–178b.

[281] Kara 1963, p. 10.

After the thirteenth century, Mo. *ǰada* was re-borrowed by several Turkic languages, thus providing the disyllabic Turkic forms, attested beginning with the Middle Turkic period: Middle Turkic: Chagh. *yada taš* '(*yamġur bončuġï derlär. bir näsnä olur, ke ägär qurban sürmäklä yamġur yaġar, ḥajar al-maṭar*) a rain bead, that is a thing of such a kind that when the blood of a sacrificial animal is smeared on it, rain ensues'[282], *ǰada tašï* '(*sang-i yada bāshad, ke ān-rā yada tāšï va yadā tāšï va yāda tāšï ham gūyand va ba-'arabī ḥajar al-maṭar bi-nāmand*) rain-stone, the same as *yada tašï* [with different spellings] and in Arabic *ḥajar al-maṭar*'[283], *yada* '(*afsūn va sang-ī* [spelt hang-i] *barā-yi bārān bar ān afsūn kunand*) magic and a stone by which magic is done for rain' (*LughT.*), *yadačï* '(*afsūngar*) magician' (*LughT.*); Ott. *yada* in *sang-i yada* 'Eskiden usûlüne göre kullanılınca yağmur yağdırdığına inanılan bir taş, yağmur taşı' in *sang-i yada* 'rain-stone'[284], *yada* '...Ve ol hacer-i bâran-esere Etrâk yada taşı ve ehl-i Fürs seng-i yada ve Arap hacerü'l-matar deyü nam-zet kıldılar ki vakt-i hacette vech-i muharrer üzere istimtar olunsa Hazret-i müsebbibü'l-esbab ol ism-i mubakerin bereketine inzâl-i matar eder'[285]; New Turkic, Kipchak: KazT *yáda* 'koldovstvo, koldun'[286], Kirgh. *ǰadaa* (an anthropological term, the same as *ǰay taš*) 'zaklinanie pogodï', *ǰadaasïn okup ǰaylagan* (folklore) 'on proiznës zaklinanie i vïzval dozhd'' *ǰadaačï*, *ǰadačï* 'the same as *ǰayčï*'[287]; Eastern: Uzb. *yada-taš* 'rain-stone'[288], *yad[a]-taš* 'rain-stone'[289], ETurki *jada~jadä* (‹ Iran.) 'rain-magic, rain-procuring; *j. taš* 'rain-stone' *jadačï* 'rain-procurer, rain-maker' *jadačïlïq* 'a rain-procurer's trade'[290], YUigh. *ǰadalan-* 'sovershat' molenie o dozhde (G. N. Potanin)'[291],

282 *Abušqa*, p. 399.

283 *Sanglakh* 205r. 21.

284 *Atai. H.* XVII, p. 37.

285 *Aks.* VII—XVIII, p. 116.

286 Damaskin 1785.

287 Yudakhin 1965, p. 210.

288 Dingel'shtedt 1893, p. 168.

289 Logofat 1913, pp. 513—4.

290 Jarring 1964, p. 145.

291 Malov 1957, p. 28.

Siberian: Alt. *d'ada*, *d'ada taš* (Teleut, Nizhne-biyskiy dialects) 'kamen', siloyu koego proizvodyat' dozhd', sneg, ili vëdro' *d'ada sös* 'zaklinanie pri étom' *d'adačï* (Nizhne-biyskiy dialect) 'zogovarivayushchiy pogodu siloyu kamnya *d'ada*' *d'adala-* (Teleut, Nizhne-biyskiy dialects) 'siloyu kamnya *d'ada* sdelat' vëdro ili nenast'e'[292], *d'ada* (Alt. Tel. Leb.) 'id.'[293]; Yakut *sata* '1.) bezoar ili bezoaroviy kamen', nakhodimïy v zheludke ili pecheni krupnïkh mlekopitayushchikh zhivotnïkh (loshadi, korovï, losya, olenya) i glukharya; po poveriyu yakutov, kamen' étot odaren volshebnoy siloy i, buduchi bïnesen na otkrïtïy vozdukh v letniy znoynïy den', proizvodit sil'nïy kholodnïy veter, buryu, dozhd' i sneg, voobshche nepogodu, nenast'e, a zimoy — teplo; takim svoystvom kamya pol'zuyutsya plovtsï, prosya poputnago vetra, ili okhotniki i zapozdavshie vesnoy putniki, kotorïe zhelali bï prodolzheniya zamorozkov; zhelaya vïzvat' buryu, nenast'e, kamen' privyazïvayut k prutu i bïstro vertyat po vozdukhu, prichem "proklinayut sebya i svoe potomstvo" (*Por.*); "po vneshnemu vidu *sata* imeet skhodstvo s figuroy cheloveka: bïvayut zametnï glaza, nos, rot" (*AK.* 59) ili predstavlyaet figuru v rod urodlivoy indyushki (*Pr.*); kamen' derzhat zavernutïm v tryapku ili shkuru lisitsï ili belki; "na Anabare rol' *sata* igraet tarbagan'ya shkurka" *AK.* 60; *kurān sata* kamen', vïzïvayushchiy zasukhu i stremitel'nïe vetrï *VS*. *Sïlgï satata* kamen', dobïtïy iz zheludka loshadi; *sata tïala* veter, proizvedenniy kamnem *sata*. 2.) prichinenie vetra i stuzhi, izmenenie pogodï posredstvom koldovstva, *B*. 3.) veter, vïzvannïy koldovstvom; burya, sil'niy veter *Ion.*; naslannïy shamanom veter i kholod *N*. *Saŋarbïta—sata bïlït buolla* rech' ego stala—chto groznoe (enastnoe) obloko'[294] *satalā-* 'puskat' *sata* dlya nenast'ya, buri, *Por.*'.[295]

[292] Verbitskiy 1884, p. 66.

[293] Radloff 1888—1911, iii, c. 207, 210.

[294] Pekarskiy 1917—30, ii, pp. 2122—3.

[295] *Op. cit*, ii, p. 2126.

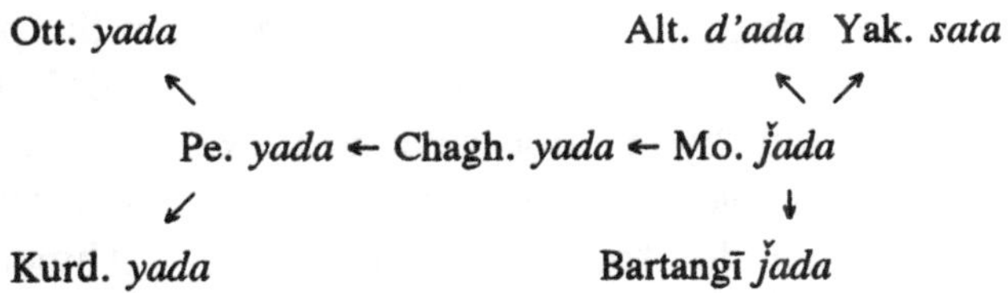

Figure 4. Mo. ǰada as a loan-word in other languages

Chaghatai has both *ǰada* and *yada*, the latter being a Turcized form, as Mo. /*ǰ*-/ was replaced by Tu. /*y*-/. The Turcized *yada* was borrowed by New Persian[296], and by Kurdish[297] probably through Persian mediation, while Bartangī *ǰada*[298] is a direct loan from Mongolian (see Fig. 4).

The final stage of the westward migration of the Mongolian word *ǰada* is Ottoman Turkish, where it appears in the Persian construction *sang-i yada* '*yada*-stone'. It is to be found only in the heavily Persized literary language, and does not occur in the vernacular or in the dialects.

The later the word appeared in the language, the greater the confusion and misunderstanding concerning its meaning in the Ottoman Turkish dictionaries. Very conveniently Barbier de Meynard[299] gives a full list of all the misunderstandings that have ever surrounded the meaning of Ott. *yede*: "serpentine, nommée aussi *yeşim* ou *beşeb*. Les anciennes tribus turques attribuaient des vertus magiques à cette pierre, surtout pour attirer le pluie. Elles en faisaient aussi des idols". Barbier de Meynard's explanation is, beyond doubt, partially based on the Ottoman

---

296 NPe. *yada* 'The magic production of an appearance of snow or rain by a certain stone; this stone itself' *yadaǰī*, *yadačī* 'One who produces rain by incantations' *yadačīgarī* 'The art of producing rain by incantations' (Steingass 1892, p. 1529).

297 Mokri 1959, p. 491.

298 Sokolova 1960, p. 120.

299 1886, p. 877.

Turkish translation of the rain-making ceremony related by Tīfāshī (quoted in Chapter 1). The meaning 'serpentine' comes from the presence of a snake in the ceremony. The confusion between *yeşim* 'jade' and *yede* is an old mistake, corrected by Pelliot several times.[300] Finally, the meaning 'idol' attributed to *yede* comes from a corrupt form *but*[301] instead of *yat* by losing one dot from under the *yod*[302]. Ahmed Vefik Paşa in his *Lehçe-i Osmani*[303], explains *yede* as follows: *yedâ aslı türki-dir. yadā tašı yeşim—kadım Türklerin yeşmden ittihâz ettikleri yağmur taşı* "*Yadâ* is genuine Turkish. The *yedâ*-stone is a jade, a rain-stone made of jade by the ancient Turks". 'Rain-stone' and 'jade' are again confused here. Finally, Sâmī[304] in his *Kâmūs-i Türki* writes: *yedâ yahut yede, yeşim denen tamarlı yeşil taş, ki eski Türkler ondan sanemlerini yaparlar ve istimtâr için suya atarlar idi* "*Yedâ* or *yede*, a streaky green stone, called *yeşim*. The ancient Turks made their idols of this [stone], and to entreat for rain they throw them into water." Here, 'rain-stone' and 'jade' are again confused, and to increase the confusion, the corrupt reading *but* 'idol' was substituted by *sanem* of the same meaning. *Yede* is the Ottoman Turkish pronunciation of Persian *yāda*; the genuine Old and Middle Turkic forms always have velar vowels.

Mo. *ǰada* was borrowed by some Kipchak, Eastern and Siberian Turkic languages, and by Yakut, (*Map* 3)—though it is not mentioned as such by Kałużyński.[305] It belongs to the older layer of Mongolian loan-words in Yakut, because Mo. /*ǰ*-/ is represented by /*s*-/.[306] In Kirghiz, both the regular *ǰay* which developed from OTu. *yād* and the Mongolian loan *ǰada* are attested.

---

[300] 1949, pp. 8–9; 1959–1963–1973, i, pp. 424–5.

[301] 'An idol, an image, any figure that is an object of adoration; etc.' (Steingass 1892, p. 154).

[302] See Köprülü Zade 1925, pp. 446–8.

[303] 1876, p. 1453.

[304] 1901, p. 1544.

[305] 1961.

[306] Kałużyński 1961, pp. 46–8.

Maps 2 and *3* show that within the Turkic linguistic area, developments of OTu. *yād* tend to survive in the central territories. They have not been attested in the west, and they have been replaced by reborrowed forms from Mongolian in the east.

Let us now return to the etymology of OTu. *yād*, or **yādă*, that has hitherto been left unexplained. As a matter of fact, Vámbéry's suggestion—namely, that OTu. *yād* is an early Iranian loan—can be accepted with some improvements. It can be ascertained that ATu. **yādă* › OTu. *yādă, yād* is a borrowing of an Eastern Middle Iranian development of OIr. *yātu*, a word attested in the Iranian languages with the meaning 'magic' and 'magician': Old Iranian: Av. *yātav-* '1) Zauberei, Behexung 2) Zauberer'[307], Middle Iranian: MPe. *jādūg [y'twk' | M ǰ'dwg, N ǰādū]* 'sorcerer, magician'[308], Sogdian *y'twk* 'magic'[309], New Iranian: NPe. *jādū* 'conjuration, magic; juggling; a conjurer'[310], Tajik *ǰodu* '1) koldovstvo, magiya; zaklinanie, zagovor; 2) charï, volshebstvo, obayanie, ocharovanie'[311] → Parachi *ǰâdū* 'sorcery, magic' *ǰâdūgar* 'sorcerer'[312]. The word *yātu* belongs to the shared Indo-Iranian heritage, see Skt. *yātú* 'sorcery, witchcraft, a kind of evil spirit, fiend, demon'.[313] In the *Rigveda*, it signifies a class of demons.[314] The term may also indicate 'sorcery'.[315]

The lending language cannot be determined with precision, but it can conveniently be termed Saka. Though the word is not attested in Khotanese Saka, OIr. *yātu* would have developed into **ǰāδa-* (nom.sg.

---

307 Bartholomae 1904, p. 1283.

308 MacKenzie 1971, p. 46.

309 Benveniste 1940.

310 Steingass 1892, p. 349.

311 *TadRS* 1954, p. 517.

312 Morgenstierne 1929, p. 261.

313 Monier—Williams 1899, p. 849.

314 Boyce 1975, p. 85.

315 Bivar 1985, p. 27.

**ǰāde̥*) in that Middle Iranian language.[316] In Khotanese Saka, the */y-/* › */ǰ-/* sound change took place before the ninth, but at the latest in the tenth century, when Khotanese documents, whose precise date is not known, were written. Consequently, both Ir. */y-/* › */ǰ/* → Tu. */ǰ-/* (in the *y*-Turkic dialects substituted by */y-/*) and Ir. */y-/* → Tu. */y-/* are theoretically possible. At any rate, in Old Turkic both the */y-/* and */ǰ-/* forms can be reckoned with. The Iranian vowel length was preserved in Old Turkic (Khakani), and was regularly lost in Middle Turkic. As far as the */-d-/* is concerned, in view of the fact that partly parallel sound changes took place in Iranian (OIr. */-t-/* › MIr. */-d-/* › */-δ-/* › NIr. */-y-/*) and in Turkic (OTu. */-d-/* › */-δ-/* › MTu. */-y-/*), it cannot be decided whether MIr. */-d-/* or */-δ-/* was borrowed by Turkic. Finally, the word final Iranian */-u/* is reflected as a reduced vowel *-ǎ* in Turkic preserved by Mo. *ǰada*, and lost in Late Old Turkic, with the possible exception of Karluk (see below).

It would seem as if the obscure and much-debated Sogdian *cδy-kr'y mrty* occurring in the *P 3* text might be satisfactorily explained. Benveniste[317] already recognized that though *cδy°* means 'charme magique'[318], on phonetic grounds it could not be explained as a continuation of IIr. *yātuka*, which otherwise occurs in the same text several times in the expected form as *y'twk*. Henning first tended to see Skt. *jala* 'water' in the Sogdian *cδy°*[319], but later he compared the Sogdian word to the "Turkic-Mongolian-Persian" *ǰadačï* and *yadačï*[320], Thus, the two eminent Iranologists agreed that *cδy-kr'y* could not satisfactorily explained

[316] OIr. */y-/* › Khot. */ǰ-/* (spelt ‹j› or ‹*gy*›), OIr. */-t-/* › Khot. */-δ-/* (spelt ‹d›), while OIr. */ā/* and */u/* remained unchanged (Gertsenberg 1981, pp. 240 and 243).

[317] 1940, p. 195, note 123.

[318] *Op. cit., Glossaire* p. 251.

[319] 1940, p. 5.

[320] 1945, p. 465; 1945a, p. 151; 1946, p. 714.

on Iranian grounds.[321] It can be assumed, therefore, that *cδy°* here is a rendering of a Turkic word, **ǰaδ*, or **ǰaδă*. Considering the very complicated relationship between the Sogdian and Turkic languages and writing-systems, it cannot be ascertained whether *cδy°* is a loan-word in Sogdian, or an occasional rendering of a word that was otherwise foreign to the Sogdians. At any rate, *cδy°* was treated as a light stem in Sogdian, and declined as such. Thus, the adopted form could have been either **ǰaδ-* or **ǰaδă*. Doerfer[322] has opted for the latter. Foreign */ǰ/* was rendered by *tsadde* in Sogdian, as in the case of the Indian loan-words.[323] On the other hand, the Turkic compound *yadčï är* that is known from Uighur[324] seems to be a calque of Sogdian *cδy-kr'y mrty /ǰaδi-karē marti/* 'the man who does *ǰaδ(ă)*'.[325]

It is difficult to identify the Turkic language or dialect from which *ǰad(ă)* of the *P 3* Sogdian text originates. However, considering the geographical and historical milieu and the remarkable role the Karluks played in the history of weather-magic in Central Asia, *ǰad(ă)* can be considered a Karluk form. In this context, the term "Karluk" is meant to cover all the Turkic dialects spoken by the subjects of the Karluk Empire because, if Pritsak[326] is right and the Karakhanids were of Karluk origin, they must have spoken a *y*-Turkic dialect. This hypothesis is supported also by another piece of evidence. According to the *Hsin T'ang shu*, the Karluks when they still lived south of the Altai in the seventh century called themselves *san-hsing yeh-hu* "the three tribes'

---

[321] Bailey (1979, p. 100) tentatively suggested that Sogd. *čδy* might be connected with Khotanese Saka *ça̱ya-* 'magic, sorcery'. Bailey's suggestion was commented on by Sims-Williams (1983a, p. 42).

[322] *Op. cit.*, p. 289.

[323] *Op. cit.* Sogd. *cnp'wδn* 'Jāmbūnada' ← North-West Prakrit *jabodaṇa-*, etc. (Sims-Williams 1983, p. 137).

[324] *MIK* III 192, line 5, see *Appendix*.

[325] On *-kr'y* see Gershevitch 1954, § 1122 and 1125.

[326] 1951.

yabghu".[327] The Chinese transcription shows a *y*-form of the Turkic title *yabġu*.

As a matter of fact, *yad(ă)* may not represent the dialect spoken by the Karluks proper, but can be considered a survival of an earlier Western Türk pronunciation. Similarly, the coexistence of *y*- and *ǰ*- forms within the Karluk Empire can be seen in the case of the Turkic title *yabġu*: according to the *Ḥudūd al-'Ālam*, "In the days of old, the kings of the Khallukh were called Jabghūy, and also Yabghū."[328] The hypothesis that *ǰad(ă)* represents a local tradition specific to the area of the Western T'ien-shan is also supported by the geographical argument to be discussed in Chapter 4.

---

[327] Ecsedy 1980, p. 28.
[328] Minorsky 1937, p. 97.

TYPES OF WEATHER-MAGIC IN INNER ASIA AND THEIR HISTORY

In the light of the testimony of written sources and the linguistic evidence, Inner Asian weather-magic may now be placed in its historical perspective. Weather-magic rites are generally rather simple and are not only specific to Inner Asian peoples; they are to be found also in other parts of the world. Still, it is possible to define certain types of weather-magic as being exclusive to certain Inner Asian ethnic groups such as the Iranians, the Turks and the Mongols. It is also possible to delineate the main trends of the historical development of these rites, and of the beliefs connected with them.

Sprinkling Water and Plunging into Water

Water plays an essential role in weather-magic, particularly in rain-making.[329] On the principle of homoeopathic magic, by throwing, sprinkling or spilling water, the rain-maker seeks to produce rain by imitating it. Various objects, connected with humidity are also used in rain-making: they are sprinkled with water or submerged in it. Finally, the rain-makers themselves seek to identify with the rain: they sprinkle each other with water, or dip into it. These ways of making rain, common throughout the world, are recounted also in the historical and the more recent material on the peoples of Inner Asia.

The sprinkling of water for the purposes of weather-magic is attested among the Iranian population of Inner Asia since the seventh century. The attendants of the Liao Emperor at the Kitan court dousing

[329] Frazer 1911, pp. 269–78.

each other with water seems to have constituted the main element of early Mongol weather-magic.

Though making rain by sprinkling water or diving into it is well attested among the Iranian population of Inner Asia and among the Kitans of the seventh to the twelfth centuries, this kind of weather-magic is not mentioned in later historical sources, and appears only occasionally in the recent descriptions. It is common only in the Volga region among the Chuvash, the Kazan Tatars and the Bashkirs, in Central Asia among the Kirghiz, and finally, among the Yellow Uighurs.

Making rain by of imitative magic is sometimes linked with animal sacrifice. In this case, water is partly substituted with the blood of the slaughtered animal. This rite occurs among the Eastern Turkis: water mixed with the blood of a red cock is sprinkled towards the sky and the four cardinal points. The historical antecedents of this rite are attested in the *Ta'rīkh-i Fakhru ʿd-Dīn Mubārakshāh* and in Chaghatai poetry in the quoted verse by ʿAlīshīr Navāʾī.

Since sprinkling water and diving into water are common to weather-magic all over the world, we hardly need to assume some historical contact to explain the Iranian, Kitan and recent Turkic rites. Yet, this way of controlling the weather is characteristic either of the Turks nor of the Mongols, the Kitans excepted.

Frogs and Snakes

Frogs and snakes are intimately associated with water, so these creatures have a widespread reputation as custodians of rain. Frazer[330] gives numerous examples from all over the world in which frogs are used in rain-charms. In the historical sources on Inner Asian weather-magic, frogs are mentioned only in the *P 3* Sogdian text[331]. As a part of a complicated

330 *Op. cit.*, pp. 292–5.

331 Benveniste 1940, pp. 59–73, lines 225–30.

rain-making ceremony, frogs are first put into fire and then wrapped in black felt and placed under water. Otherwise, frogs are mentioned in neither the other historical sources nor the recent anthropological descriptions, apart from a reference by Malov to a malign charm practised by the Taranchis of the Ili River Valley. Here, an incantation is said over a live frog that is being pricked to death with a needle. The dead frog is then buried under the gate of the person on whom the spell has been cast. Neither the charm nor the frog seem to have anything to do with weather-magic, however. The incantation said is called *yada,* which otherwise always means 'weather-magic' in Eastern Turki. It can be presumed, thus, that the role of frogs in malign charm is only secondary; originally, they may have been used in rain-charm.

On the other hand, frogs play an essentials role in recent Indian rain-making ceremonies. Frazer provides several examples[332] and there is also a curious hymn in the *Rigveda*, the so-called "frog-hymn", which seems to be a rain-charm.[333] Furthermore, frogs appear in the *P 3* Sogdian text in the typical Indian milieu provided by the Nāgas, the serpent genii personifying the terrestrial waters of the lakes, ponds, rivers and seas. The purpose of roasting the frog is probably to provoke the supernatural powers to come to the aid of the frog, custodian of rain, by providing the longed-for precipitation. There are several examples from different parts of India of frogs being exposed to heat to provoke rain.[334] The significance of wrapping the frog into black felt is not very clear; felt is usually used in weather-magic to stop the rain or a storm. In sum, the presence of frogs in rain-making can best be understood as an Indian contribution to the history of weather-magic in Inner Asia.

Snakes are used to stop the rain in the few examples quoted by Frazer[335], and they are mentioned in some historical sources in connection

---

332 1911, pp. 293–5.

333 Bloomfield 1896.

334 Frazer, *op. cit.*, pp. 293–4.

335 *Op. cit.*, pp. 295–6.

with Inner Asian weather-magic. In recent anthropological accounts, snakes are reported only in Anatolia, among the Turks of Turkey and the Turkmens who burn them to make rain.[336] Concerning the Mongol peoples, snakes are attested among the Ordos Mongols (*mogoin džada*) and among the Kalmucks in a distinctly Buddhist milieu.

The earliest mention of a complicated rain-making rite in which snakes appear is the *P 3*[337] Sogdian text in which—along with other animals—a snake is hung head down. The same motif occurs much later, in the thirteenth century rain-charm performed by a Turkic weather-magician in the army of the sovereign of Khwārazm, ʿAlāʾ al-Dīn Muḥammad. The ceremony described by Tīfāshī is rather complicated, and consists of several elements, of which the use of rain-stones will be discussed below. According to Tīfāshī, the weather-magician placed a bowl full of water on the ground of a roofless tent pitched for the rain-making ceremony, built a stand of three reeds over the bowl, then fixed the tail of a snake to the horizontal reed, letting the animal hang with its head down over the bowl full of water. There was some distance left between the head of the animal and the surface of the water. The use of rain-stones followed.

This description of rain-making provides the key to a better understanding of the phrase *luu üntürgüči yadčï* that occurs in an Old Uighur confession of sins[338], a text in which one can expect to find heathen Old Turkic religious practices among the sins to be confessed. The hitherto not fully understood *luu üntürgüči yadčï* is mentioned in the list of disreputable professions, whose practice involved the killing of animals and human beings, or causing harm and sufferings to them. The translation of the passage is based on the better-preserved *TT IV*:

---

[336] Acıpayamlı 1963–64, p. 18.

[337] Lines 245–60.

[338] The text is known in two slightly differing variants, the first edited by Müller (1910) in *Uigurica II*, pp. 84–89, the second by Bang and Gabain (1930) in *Türkische Turfantexte IV*, pp. 1–20.

And if we, Il and Tüzmiš, have committed the twelve sins called *asanvir*[339] sins and evil deeds from time immemorial, if, for example, we have become butchers who kill sheep, if we have become poultry-keepers, if we have become hunters of wild boars, fishermen, hunters of stags and wild game, and trappers, if we have become netters, bird-snarers, falconers, if we have become killers of living creatures that fly or crawl on their bellies, if we have become sellers of dog-meat, if we have become killers of the *ačakram*-snake, if we have become weather-magicians who raise snakes, if we have become torturers and gaolers of [four-footed] creatures, if we have become executioners who kill human beings, and if we have committed these twelve *asanvir* sins, and we have sundered [living beings] from their lives with a merciless heart, and have caused them suffering, and killed them, we now repent, and realize that we have sinned.[340]

---

[339] Sanskrit *a-saṃvara* 'not to be concealed' (Monier—Williams 1899, p. 117).

[340] *(53) ymä mn il tüz-miš birlä ilki-siz-dä-bärü iki ygrmi (54) türlüg asanvir atlγ tsui ayaγ qïlïnč qïltïmz ärsär (55) inčä qaltï qoyn ölürgüči tuž-i boltumuz ärsär taqïγu (56) igidgüči boltumuz ärsär tonguzčï balïqčï käyikči angčï tuz(57)-aqčï boltumuz ärsär torčï čïvγačï quščï itärči učuγma (58) baγrïn yorïγma tïnlγ-larïγ ölürgüči boltumuz ärsär it (59) ätin satγučï boltumuz ärsär ačakram yïlan ölürgüči (60) boltumuz ärsär luu üntürgüči yadčï boltumuz ärsär ////q///(61)-larïγ qïnaγučï boqaγučï boltumuz ärsär kiši ölürgüči čantal (62) boltumuz ärsär bu iki ygrmi türlüg asanvarukikilar išin (63) išlägüči bolup yrlïqančsïz köngülin isig öz-lärintä adïrdï (64)-mz ämgätdimz ölürdümz ärsär ạmti anï barča ökünür-biz yaz(65)-uqumuz-nï bilinür-biz* (parallel text in Müller 1910, pp. 84—5, lines 6—18).

The phrase *luu üntürgüči yadčï* was translated by Müller[341] as "ein Nāgas aufsteigen machender Zauberer", and for lack of anything better, he interpreted the phrase as the Turkic translation of the Indian snake-charmer ("Schlangenbeschwörer"). Bang and Gabain[342] accepted this translation, in part. However, they regarded *luu üntürgüči yadčï* as two different professions ("Schlangenbeschwörer" *und* "Zauberer") in the list of disreputable occupations.[343] However, this interpretation does not fit into the structure of the text. All the professions listed are connected with animals; consequently, *luu üntürgüči* should be understood as an attribute of *yadčï* "the weather-magician who causes snakes to rise" in a construction similar to *qoyn ölürgüči tuži* "the butcher who kills sheep" and *kiši ölürgüči čantal*[344] "the executioner who kills human beings".[345]

---

[341] 1911, p. 84.

[342] 1930, p. 9.

[343] Similarly, Clauson (1972, p. 763), under *lu* 'snake charmer and magician'.

[344] Sanskrit *caṇḍāla* 'an outcast, man of the lowest and most despised of the mixed tribes' (Monier-Williams 1899, p. 383).

[345] Bang disagreed with Müller's explanation already in 1915 (pp. 623–4) when the better preserved *TT IV* version of the text was still not known. He argued, that the number of sins was indicated in the text, and to achieve the desired number, *luu üntürgüči* and *yadčï* should have been counted separately. Unfortunately, Bang—following Müller (1910, p. 85)—misunderstood the *iki ygrmi türlüg asanvir atlγ tsui ayaγ qïlïnč* as 'eighteen kinds of sins and evil deeds' for twelve, so thus the whole argumentation is erroneous, because he was looking for eighteen sins instead of twelve. His hypothesis was not accepted by Pelliot (1930, p. 301) for other reasons. As a matter of fact, if the species of animals and the ways of killing or torturing living beings are considered, they, in fact, amount to twelve: (1) the butchers who kill sheep (2) poultry-keepers (3) hunters of wild boars (4) fishermen (5) hunters of stags and wild game (Hend.) (6) trappers (7) netters and bird-snarers (Hend.), namely, fowlers (8) falconers (9) sellers of dog-meat (10) killers of the *ačakram*-snake (11) weather-magicians who raise snakes and (12) executioners who kill human beings.

Thus Müller's translation is correct; the noun-phrase *luu üntürgüči* is an attribute of *yadčï*, and the weather-magician really does cause the snake to rise. True, in the way that the Indian snake-charmer does, but as described in the rain-making ceremony recounted by Tīfāshī. To sum up: there seems to have been some kind of weather-magic performed by means of snakes among the Uighurs. The ceremony, unknown in its details, was presumably comparable to that performed at the court of the Khwārazmshāhs.

Qibchāqī recounts another method of rain-making originating in Khwārazm: a rain-stone is placed on a piece of cotton, and a snake's or a rat's throat is cut over the rain-stone while a charm is murmured in Khwārazmian. The Nāgas are also mentioned in a Lamaist Kalmuck weather-magic rite recounted by Pallas.

In the few examples given by Frazer, snakes are used to stop the rain; in Inner Asian instances, however, we see the snake used to make rain. In all the examples mentioned, both historical and recent, snakes as a means of rain-making occur among Turkic peoples and in regions where there is a remarkable Iranian influence. Thus, we can conjecture that in the rain-making ceremony recounted by Qibchāqī, the use of a snake is in keeping with some local Iranian tradition. We have seen that, in Indian mythology the serpent genii, the *Nāgas*, personify the terrestrial waters. The *Nāgas* are invoked in the *P 3* Sogdian text, too, to bring rain and dew with the wind. On the other hand, snakes are not mentioned in descriptions of recent Inner Asian Turkic and Mongol relevant customs. For the time being, we must assume that in all the known cases of rain-making the use of snakes in weather-magic is an Indian, or perhaps Iranian import adopted by some of the Turkic peoples. We might note that the two rain-making ceremonies of possibly Iranian origin in which snakes are used show other similarities as well. Both take place under a provisional shelter: according to the Sogdian text, a twenty-five-headed tent (*xrγ'xh*) is erected, while the Khwārazmian ceremony was performed in a roofless tent. Both are presumably models of the Universe.

The meaning of the use of snakes in rain-making can perhaps be explained through analogy with Indian examples. When rain is needed in

Northwestern India, a frog is hung head up on a tall bamboo tree for a day or two. The notion is that the god of rain, seeing the frog in trouble, will take pity on it and send the rain.[346] Considering the fact that snakes, as seen in the case of the Nāgas, are also closely associated with water, it can be surmised that snakes are killed (by the Khwārazmians), hung with their heads down (by the Sogdians), raised (by the Uighurs), hung over water, but without touching it (by the Khwārazmians), and thrown into fire (by the Turks of Turkey and the Turkmens) following the same principle. In short, depriving snakes of their natural element, water, or placing them into unnatural positions is meant to bring about rain.

THE DARK-COLOURED HORSE

Animals, particularly when black, occur in rain-charms all over the world, and they do so in Turkic weather-magic as well. Somewhat surprisingly, to my knowledge this feature of Inner Asian weather-magic has never been discussed or even mentioned in the otherwise vast literature on the subject.

The horse, the most important domestic animal of the Inner Asian nomads, is used in weather-magic by several Turkic peoples. In the historical sources, weather-magic performed by means of a dark-coloured horse is mentioned in the *P 3* Sogdian text. The *cδw-kr'y mrty*, that is, the weather-magician, paints his face black, mounts a dark-coloured horse and, holding the reins to which vulture and pheasant feathers have been fixed[347], turns seven times towards the east, then again seven times towards the west while shouting loudly three times. This ceremony constitutes only a part of the complicated rite which produces heavy rain. In the recent descriptions, the Eastern Turki weather-magician mounts a horse and makes it gallop; it is thus that he is believed to make rain on

[346] Frazer 1911, p. 293.

[347] Lines 230–9.

the mane of the horse, and snow on its back. A few sources relate that the Altai Turks make snow by mounting a horse, whistling and shouting all the while.

Weather-magic by means of dark or dark spotted horses can, as we shall see, be understood in terms of homoeopathic or imitative magic. In the imagination of the Inner Asian Turks, horses, particularly dark or dark spotted horses, stand for dark coloured rain or snow clouds, the horse galloping along the steppe being associated with clouds driven by the wind. This explanation is supported by the metaphors used in the "Kazak" part of an Eastern Turki *yadači-kitab*, in which black horses are clearly identified with black clouds. Following the law of similarity, the rain-maker proposes to make the dark-coloured rain clouds bring rain by galloping a dark-coloured horse identified with the clouds.

Weather-magic performed by means of dark-coloured horses is attested in Sinkiang and in the region of the Altai Mountains. The rite has survived in an altered form as a children's game, among the Turkmens of Iraq. A young lad or a child disguises himself as a horse, with horse ears and a tail, and hops and jumps along the streets of the village. The colour of the "horse" is again significant: the youngster playing the horse paints his face black. The Bashkir name for the rain-stone, *kolon taš* 'colt-stone', can perhaps also be interpreted as the survival of a rain-making rite performed by means of a horse, mixed with beliefs connected to the rain-stone.

The fact that rain-making by means of a dark-coloured horse exists, if only in the form of a children's game, among the Turkmens of Iraq who live far from the regions where this kind of weather-magic is attested, allows us to suppose that this practice goes back a long way among the Turks. This supposition is confirmed by the way rain is made by the *cδw kr'y mrty* in the *P 3* Sogdian text, which can, thus, be regarded as the Turkic component among the weather-magic rites occurring in the Sogdian text.

Furthermore, though black animals, such as black horses, are used in rain-making rites all over the world, mounting and galloping dark-coloured horses associated with dark-coloured clouds appears to be a specifically Turkic rite. It is, in fact, the "Turkic" way *par excellence* of doing weather-magic. It is interesting that this rite is not attested among the Mongols.

In the "Kirghiz" part of Eastern Turki, the *yadači-kitab,* the rain-maker, not only mounts a black horse, but also dons a black cap and clothing. The black garb is interpreted as a sign of mourning in the text, a misunderstanding of the origins of the rite. In the "Tibetan" part of the same Eastern Turki *yadači-kitab*, the rain-maker puts on black armour and mounts a black horse. The custom that all participants at a Chuvash rain-making ceremony wear black, while white clothes are strictly prohibited should be understood in the same way. Black clothes in all these cases are meant to recall the black colour of the clouds. The fact that the rain-maker paints his face black in the *P 3* Sogdian text is to be interpreted in the same way.

The Rain-Stone

If dipped in water or sprinkled with it stones are often believed capable to produce rain, snow and storms. This kind of use of stones in weather-magic can also be considered a particular case of rain-making by means of water. Frazer[348] gives several examples of such a use of stones in rain-charms from five continents. Rain-stones play an essential part in the great bulk of the historical and anthropological sources on Turkic and Mongol weather-magic. The rain-making ceremony itself, however, is rather simple, and, for the most part, follows one and the same pattern: the rain-stones are dipped into water or sprinkled with it, though this rite may constitute only a part of a more complicated ceremony. The differences among the rites and the connected beliefs lie mainly in the peculiarities of the rain-stones.

---

[348] 1911, pp. 304–11.

THE DISTINCTIVE FEATURES OF RAIN-STONES

Let us now summarize the peculiarities of rain-stones according to recent beliefs (see *Fig. 5*). For technical reasons the chart is incomplete. For example, rain-stones have sometimes been found in caves (by the Uzbeks and the Altai Turks), a fact not indicated in the chart.

	a piece of stone				
	mineral			bezoar	
	ordinary stone transformed by a ritual	special stone		in human beings	in animals
		crystal	celestial phenomena		
Turkish	+				
Azeri	+				
Turkmen	+				
Noghai				+	+
Bashkir	+				+
Kazak			+		+
Kirghiz	+				+
Uzbek	+		+		
ETurki			+		+
Altai Turks	+				+
Tuvin		+			+
Yakut		+	+	+	+
Buriat			+		+
Oirot					+
Kalmuck					+
Ordos					+

Figure 5. Distinctive features of the rain-stone among the Turks and the Mongols

The word "stone" has been used in the foregoing in a rather general sense, both as a mineral, and as a thing resembling a stone, *e.g.* a hard concretion in the body of living beings. As a matter of fact, this is the first distinction that must be made: some Altaic peoples use particular kinds of minerals, while others use bezoar stones as rain-stones in weather-magic. *Fig. 5* shows that minerals tend to be used exclusively by the Turks in the west (by the Oghuz). Otherwise, minerals are used in weather-magic along with bezoars among the other Turkic peoples from the Bashkirs and the Kazaks to the distant Yakuts. The exception to this generalization is the case of the Noghais. The relevant information is drawn from ʿAbduʾl-Karīm Bukhārī's account. Speaking of the rain-stone of the Eastern Turkis, he mentions that such stones are also used by the Noghai Tatars of the Crimea. They can be found in the heads of human beings, of pigs, horses and other animals. Thus the rain-stone of the Noghais was beyond doubt a bezoar. Though the Noghai name for the rain-stone is not known from the account, in view of the fact that the Noghais have long been under a strong influence of the neighbouring Kalmucks, whose weather-magic is dominated by the use of bezoars, it is safe to assume that their use among the Noghais is the result of Kalmuck influence.

Otherwise the use of bezoars in weather-magic is peculiar to the Mongols. Only the Buriats believe that a rain-stone may appear as a result of a fulgurite falling into water.

Not only is the use of bezoars as rain-stones predominant among the Mongol peoples of recent times, but according to the earliest known (Chinese) sources, they were so used by the Mongols at the time of the Yüan Dynasty. Consequently, the use of bezoar-stones may be considered to be the Mongol contribution to Inner Asian weather-magic.

Stones found in the intestines, and particularly in the stomachs, of animals and human beings have often been held to possess magical properties. In the Middle East, they were used as antidotes and medicine by the Arabs and the Persians. They were likewise known to the Chinese who, for example, set bezoar-stones in rings that were sucked against poisons. The use of bezoars in weather-magic, however, is unique to the Mongols.[349]

The use of the bezoar can be understood in terms of contagious magic. Bezoar-stones develop in the intestines of animals where they are in constant contact with humidity. Consequently, they are closely associated in people's minds with humidity and water, and are thus believed to possess the property of producing rain if placed in water. According to the beliefs of some Turkic and Mongol peoples, the rain-stone is effective only for a limited time; then it loses its power and "dies". However, it can be revitalized by certain methods. The Eastern Turkis believe that when the magical power of the *yada*-stone begins to diminish, it should immediately be dipped into blood, or given to a red cock or to an old he-goat to swallow. Recovered from the intestines of the red cock or the old billy goat after a time, the rain-stone regains its efficacy. The *yada*-stone does not lose its power at all if wrapped in a blue piece of cloth or kept in a humid place. The Yakuts preserve the power of the rain-stone by wrapping it in the hide of the animal from which it was taken. According to the Mongol Uriankhais, the rain-stone is active for three years, but it can be revitalized if an animal of the kind from which the bezoar was taken is wounded, and the rain-stone is placed so as to catch the breath of the dying animal. The bezoar will not lose its power at all if it is kept wrapped in the hide or feathers of an animal of the kind from which it was taken. All these examples show that the power of the bezoar to produce rain derives from its being continuously in contact with humidity in the intestines of living beings.

As can be seen, the bezoar-stone has been used in Mongol weather-magic at least from the time of the earliest sources, that is roughly from the thirteenth century on. Among the Turkic peoples, the use of the bezoar as a rain-stone is attested among some Kipchak

---

[349] Frazer (1911, p. 305) gives two examples for the use of the bezoar in weather-magic, the first concerns the Mongols, the second the Yakuts, the latter case being due to Mongol influence, as will be seen below.

(Bashkir, Kirghiz and Kazak), Eastern (Eastern Turki) and Siberian Turkic peoples. In the case of each of these peoples, however, the use of the bezoar coexists with the utilization for the same purpose of other kinds of stones as well. Regrettably, the historical sources on Turkic weather-magic are silent about the peculiarities of the rain-stones. At any event, we are never told that the rain-stone is a bezoar. On the contrary, the Islamic legend on the rain-stones in the mountain pass in the land of the Karluks suggests that they lay on the ground, since felt had to be tied around the hooves of the riding and pack-animals in order not to hit one of them and thus cause a storm. Boyle[350] has tentatively suggested that the rain-stones used by the Turks in the ninth and tenth centuries were bezoars.[351] However, Boyle's suggestion is based on late Mongol data. The only exception he refers to is the legend of the origin of the rain-stones from the mountains of the east, in which some animals pick up stones of which they have inspired knowledge. Each animal takes a stone into its mouth, raises its head towards the heavens, and thus produces clouds for protection from the excessive heat of the land of the rising sun. The stones taken into their mouths by the animals in this story are not to be confused with bezoars. Whatever the rain-stones are, they are clearly picked up by the animals off the ground.

The earliest source on the origin of rain-stones, Tīfāshī's treatise on mineralogy written before 1253, makes no mention of the bezoar; when Tīfāshī's work was copied in later centuries, the bezoar-stone was added to Tīfāshī's text. For example, Muḥammad ibn Mansūr Shīrāzī, in his *Risāla-i jawahir* written in the second half of the fifteenth century and based on Tīfāshī's treatise, tells the story of the rain-making ceremony performed at the court of the Khwārazmshāh ʿAlāʾ al-Dīn Muḥammad, and adds that the rain-stones may be minerals from China, or may originate in the stomachs of pigs. Then there follows the story of the origin of rain-stones taken from Tīfāshī. To my knowledge, mention

[350] 1972, pp. 187–8 and p. 192.

[351] Similarly, Roux 1984, p. 96.

of the bezoar as a rain-stone occurs only in post-thirteenth century sources, only after the Mongol conquest.

In the chapter on the linguistic argument, I indicated that *ǰada*, the Mongol word for 'weather magic', can be found as a loan word in Chaghatai, Kazan Tatar, Kirghiz, Uzbek, Eastern Turki, Yellow Uighur, Altai Turkic and Yakut from the Middle Turkic period on. *Maps 3* and *4* show that the use of bezoars and the occurrence of the Mongol loan word *ǰada* roughly coincide. Since we know from historical sources that weather-magic had been performed by means of certain rain-stones among the Turks from early times, it is safe to assume that at the time of the Mongol conquest, a new "technique" was introduced to Turkic weather-magic: the use of bezoars instead of other rain-stones that had been utilized before Mongol times. The Mongol word *ǰada* was borrowed by the Turks along with the new technique.

The question now remains what kind of rain-stones were used by the Turks before the adoption of the bezoar from the Mongols. As we have seen, early historic sources on the rain-stones of the Turks do not provide any direct information on the specifics of these stones. The earliest source on how to find a rain-stone is Tīfāshī's treatise: rain-stones can be found in the soil under the nests of the ruddy goose (*Casarca ferruginea*) called *surkhāb* in Persian. This bird is the size of a goose, and has red feathers. It lives in China and in Eastern Iran in the territories neighbouring China. When there are abundant rains, and the water level is high, the *surkhāb* builds its nest on island marshlands. When the water ebbs, rain-stones of the size of an egg can be found under the nests of the *surkhāb* at a depth of two ells. They are pulverulent and ash-coloured or white with red spots. The connection between the nests of the *surkhāb* and the rain-stones can again be understood in terms of contagious magic. While the nests of the water-birds are flooded, the stones they are built on are also under water. Thus, the stones are believed to be able to produce water any time later if they are dipped into water again. There is one piece of evidence that admits of a similar explanation. According to the beliefs of the Altai Turks, the rain-stone (*d'ada-taš*) can be found among rocks exposed to constant wind. Based on the law of contact, it is believed that wind can be produced by means of this stone.

Occasionally, birds play a role in rain-magic.[352] Sparrows are drowned in the sacrificial food by the Chuvash, and there is a vague reference to some kind of long-legged big bird, probably a grallatorial bird, in connection with the Kirghiz of Sinkiang. The role of water-fowl can also be understood again in terms of contagious magic: they are in continuous contact with water: consequently, water can be produced by their instrumentality.

Be that as it may, the way of finding rain-stones related by Tīfāshī has no parallel in later Turkic material, so it can hardly serve for the reconstruction of the original distinctive features of the stones used in Turkic weather-magic. It seems, rather, to be an allusion to some local, perhaps Iranian, beliefs.

Fig. 5 shows the peculiarities of rain-stones, both minerals and bezoars. The former are distinguished from ordinary stones by supernatural qualities acquired in some ritual, in most cases, having a prayer or a spell said over them. In various parts of Turkey, prayers are said or verses from the Koran are recited over ordinary pieces of stone thrown into water. The Azeris pray by rivers, and drop a piece of stone into a bag after each prayer before they throw the bag filled with the stones into a dried-up riverbed. The Turkmens also recite verses from the Koran over stones to endow them with magical properties. The Kirghiz transform ordinary pieces of stone into rain-stones by forty days of prayer and some magical rite that takes place in water.[353] All these ways of getting a rain-stone are more or less tinged with Islamic ritual.

However, Turkic rain-stones possess some other distinctive features that are listed in the second and third columns of *Fig. 5*. According to the beliefs of the Kazaks, rain and storm can be produced

---

[352] Frazer 1911, p. 287.

[353] In the case of the Bashkirs, it is not known what distinguishes the rain-stone from ordinary stones.

by means of the *ǰaytasï*, the 'thunderbolt-stone'. The Uzbeks believe that the place of occurrence of the *yad[a]*-stone can be recognized by the beams of light flashing out of the ground. The Eastern Turkis of Guma believe that the *yada*-stone falls from heaven in the autumn. The Tuvins use as rain-stones rock-crystals in which clouds can be seen, and some of the Yakut rain-stones are also crystals. According to the Yakuts, one kind of *sata* can be found in the early morning under trees struck by lightning. There is also an interesting Mongol belief: according to the Buriats, a rain-stone comes into being if fulgurite falls into water. It seems that in all these cases, rain-stones are somehow connected with light and/or celestial phenomena. They emit light, or, being crystals, reflect the clouds in the sky. They fall from heaven, or are associated with lightning, in this latter case, again being connected with light.

The belief that the stone through which weather can be changed has to do with lightning has been preserved by the Kazak language in a curious way. In Kazak, *ǰay* (<OTu. *yād*) means 'lightning', thus *ǰaytasï* literary means 'a lightning-stone' or the like. This shift of meaning from OTu. *yād* 'weather-magic' can only be explained by assuming some kind of semantic link between the lightning and the stone used in weather-magic. The same notion is attested among the Yakuts, where one sort of rain-stone is the *eting-satata*, *i.e.* the 'thunderbolt-*sata*'. Generally speaking, it seems that all beliefs concerning the origin or distinguishing features of rain-stones are somehow connected with celestial or atmospheric phenomena: light, lightning and thunderbolts.

It can be assumed that these Turkic beliefs are survivals of the original Old Turkic notions on rain-stones. We can account for them in terms of contagious magic: weather, *i.e.* atmospheric phenomena, can be influenced by means of a stone that itself is connected with atmospheric phenomena. In the course of time, these authentic Turkic beliefs were overshadowed by later Mongol influence in the case of some Turkic peoples, though among the Bashkirs, the Kazaks, the Kirghiz, the Eastern Turkis, the Altai Turks, the Tuvins and the Yakuts both the earlier Turkic, and the later Mongol beliefs concerning the specifics of a rain-stone occur. Among the Eastern Turkis of Guma, the two sets of notions have been amalgamated: the *yada*-stone falls from heaven in the autumn. It falls on a lucerne field, or on any green field, is eaten by an ox, and some time later can be recovered from its stomach. In this story, two different notions have been reconciled. The primal concept, the celestial origin of the rain-stone, has been retained, and an adequate explanation has been found for its presence in the stomach of an ox. This is the later, Mongol notion of the origin of the rain-stone, one borrowed by the Eastern Turkis along with the Mongol loan word *yada*.

When not in use the rain-stone has to be kept hidden, as it may cause harm to people other than the weather-magician, particularly to foreigners who are not allowed to use it. According to the beliefs of the Kirghiz, if someone accidentally finds a lost rain-stone, he may be struck by poverty, illness and death. The rain-stones are, for this reason, always carefully secluded by their owners, and the weather-magician even buries his rain-stone under ground when he feels his death is near. Similarly, the Yakuts believe that the *sata*-stone must be kept hidden in a leather-bag by its owner. It can be taken out only in case of necessity, as it loses its power if it is seen by foreigners, or is touched by a woman. The belief that the rain-stone should be kept with care is also mentioned in an Uighur text: "If the [weather-magician] wants to perform weather-magic, he should keep the [rain-stone] to himself carefully. If he does not do so, he exposes himself to serious danger."[354]

THE RITE

Before going on to reconstruct the weather-making rites of the ancient Turks, we might mention here that in recent Turkic weather-making ceremonies among the Eastern Turkis, the use of the rain-stone coexists with the dark-coloured horse motif. When Eastern Turkis prepare for a long journey, they buy a bezoar and give it to an *aχun*, who weaves a net

---

[354] *[..........] yad yadlayïn tisär ät'özin [...]γ küzädm[iš krgäk] . ät'özin küzädmäsär uluγ ada-qa tušar. (MIK III 192,* lines 2–4, see Appendix).

of black horse's hair, and while reciting a spell over the bezoar, wraps it in the net. There is also a rain-making ceremony in which the *yada*-stone fixed to horsehair is dangled into water. A final connection is that the rain-stone can be revitalized by fixing it to a black horse's tail.

In the first two cases, the rain-making ceremony can be analyzed as a sentence with two motifs. On the principle of similarity, the employment of black horsehair is meant to make the black rain-clouds come, while dipping the rain-stone into water is intended to produce rain.

The Old Turkic weather-making rites performed by means of rain-stones can be reconstructed on the basis of information scattered in Islamic sources, interpreted in the light of anthropological data. Jābir ibn Ḥayyān (seventh century) reports that rain-stones are placed in a wash tub full of water and rubbed together. Relying on Marwazī (ninth century), Yāqūt recounts, that if the Turks want rain, they move their rain-stones slightly in the air. If they need snow and hail, they intensify the movement. Bīrūnī claims himself to have witnessed a Turkic rain-making ceremony: the Turkic rain-maker dipped the rain-stones into water, then he threw the water in which the stones had been soaked towards the sky, while he murmured and cried out. Heavy rains were also expected to ensue if the rain-stones were knocked against each other, or were rubbed. The story of the mountain pass in the land of the Karluks suggests that if certain stones in that pass were knocked together by the hooves of the riding and pack-animals passing through, dark mist and heavy rains followed.

The Old Turkic rites have parallels in recent Turkic weather-magic. The custom of dipping stones in water occurs among the modern Turkic peoples from Anatolia as far as Eastern Siberia. To produce rain, the Eastern Turki weather-magician holds the bezoar, fixed to a withe, above his head in the air. Some Oghuz living in Iran knock stones against each other to make rain. The Kirghiz mullas pray for rain holding the rain-stones in their hands. The Yakuts believe that if the *sata*-stone kept in the palm is lifted towards the sky, a cold wind begins to blow. If the rain-stone is turned towards the sun and is knocked on, winds are expected to blow the following day.

The description Bīrūnī gives of a Turkic rain-making ceremony originating from the mountain pass in the land of the Karluks consists of three segments, which make it unique in the literature. The segments are the following: the rain-maker wades into water—the meaning of the rite is to produce rain according to the law of similarity;[355] he puts a rain-stone into his mouth—the only human action of this sort mentioned in the sources; and he moves his hands. We find something of a parallelin the story of the origin of the rain-stone from the mountains of the East, where certain animals take rain-stones into their mouths to conjure up clouds and thus protect themselves against the excessive heat of the sun. We can assume that the reality behind this legend was precisely the weather-magician's practice of taking the rain-stone into his mouth as described in Bīrūnī's account. The motif of *animals* taking the rain-stones into their mouths seems to be a product of scholarly speculation by Islamic authors who may not have understood the meaning of the rite. It has been suggested that the legend of the rain-stone in the mountain-pass in the land of the Karluks and the legend on the origin of the rain-stone from the mountains of the East are two variants of one and the same earlier legend.

As we have already seen, to produce rain, the rain-stone needs to be in contact with water. The motif of the rain-maker's taking the rain-stone into his mouth can possibly be understood in the same way, with saliva substituting for water. Each of the first two segments in the rain-making ceremony recounted by Bīrūnī are, thus, meant to produce rain by means of homoeopathic magic.

The third motif is the rain-maker's waving his hands. It is, again, an instance of imitative magic: by waving his hands he is conjuring up the wind that will bring the rain-clouds. Similar allusions occur in the *P 3* Sogdian text. The weather-magician, having mounted his horse, shakes the reins to which pheasant and vulture feathers have been fixed to call upon the wind. The rain-making ceremony performed by means of rain-stones originating from the mountain-pass in the land of the Karluks, thus,

---

355 Frazer 1911, pp. 277–8.

consists of two segments meant to produce rain, and of one segment meant to conjure up wind. Descriptions of similar rites have been adduced above from recent Eastern Turki anthropological literature.

The Old Turkic sources contain no references to the rites themselves. Even Maḥmūd al-Kāshgharī, who himself witnessed a rain-making ceremony among the Yaghmas, does not recount the ceremony itself. The only scraps of information on rain-making rites in Turkic sources are in two badly mutilated Old Uighur texts (see Appendix). They describe that rain-stones are rubbed together (*ymä yad tašlarïn sürtüp*)[356], and that they must be washed by the *yadčï är* three times a month (*yad tašïn bir ay üč [qata] [ät]özin yumïš krgäk*).[357] Thus, we find our conclusions on Old Turkic rain-making ceremonies drawn from Islamic sources supported by genuine Old Turkic evidence.

THE USE OF RAIN-STONES: THE FUNCTIONAL ASPECT

In most of the historical sources (Jābir ibn Ḥayyān, Bīrūnī, the *P 3* Sogdian text and Tīfāshī), weather-magic performed by means of the rain-stone aims at producing rain. The importance of sufficient rainfall in the arid areas of Inner Asia requires no explanation. However, Maḥmūd al-Kāshgharī recounts an unusual instance of producing rain for the purpose of putting out a fire.

There are a few recorded instances when excessive rain, sometimes attributed to overly effective weather-magic, must be stopped. Such was the aforementioned case of the Khwārazmshāhs. Generally speaking, the rain can be stopped by reversing the rite which made it fall. According to the *P 3* Sogdian text, the rain-stone is to be taken out of water. Rain can be stopped and warm and sunny weather procured by means of the rain-stone according to the beliefs of several modern Turkic peoples. The Eastern Turkis believe that if the *yada*-stone is put in a

---

356 *TT II S 501 (U 3004)*, line 4.

357 *MIK III 192*, lines 6–7.

warm place, the sun will appear. Similarly, the Altai Turks place the rain-stone in a dry and hot place to produce clear weather: for example, the rain-stone is fixed to a stick, and hung over a fire.

Another function of Altaic weather-magic is to conjure up foul weather, wind, storm, hail and snow, in order to confound the enemy. The earliest instance of cold wind and snow being called up occurs in connection with the events relating an Uighur military campaign lead against the Tibetans in 765. There were some "magicians" (in Chinese *wu*) in the Uighur army who produced the bad weather. The story implies that the Uighur weather-magician could confine the effects of the bad weather to the place where the enemy was located, for only the Tibetans were struck by the tempest and were made unable to fight. Though the *Chiu T'ang shu* does not mention what kind of ceremony the Uighurs performed, relying on Tamīm ibn Baḥr's account of the "pebbles of the Toghuzghuz [*i.e.* Uighur] kings with which they bring down rain, snow and cold", it can be assumed that in Uighur weather-magic rain-stones were used also for military purposes.

In the western parts of Inner Asia, the Islamic sources report on the magical stones producing rain, hail, snow and storms of the Türks, the Oghuz, the Toghuzoghuz and of the Karluks. Though Yāqūt, quoting Marwazī, remarks that the Turks can do serious harm to their enemies by means of these "pebbles", there is no direct reference in the early Islamic sources to the use of the rain-stones in warfare. However, there are accounts of weather-magic being used in warfare by the Turks. One of these accounts, on the Sāmānid campaign against the Karluks, is told by Yāqūt, who claimed that weather-magic was used against the enemy by the Turks in the way described in the *Chiu T'ang shu*. The passage quoted from the *Shāhnāma* reveals that the Turks, too, were known in Sāmānid Iran to have used weather-magic in warfare. In the events described by Yāqūt and recounted in the *Shāhnāma* in a literary form, the Turks probably worked their weather-magic with rain-stones.

The fragmentary Old Uighur manuscripts edited in the Appendix and Kāshgharī's *Dīwān* provide the first occurrences of *yād* (> Khakani *yāt*), the Old Turkic word meaning 'weather-magic'. It seems that this

Turkic word generally, though not exclusively, denotes weather-magic performed by means of rain-stones. Kāshgharī clearly says that *yāt* is "a type of divination using special stones". It may also be assumed that at least in some of the cases, these stones are identical to the "pebbles" used in warfare. Before extrapolating these conclusions to examples of Turkic weather-magic of earlier periods, however, first of all, let us consider the geographical argument for rain-stones (called *yād* in Old Turkic) having been used as a tactical device in warfare.

THE GEOGRAPHICAL ARGUMENT AND THE EARLY HISTORY OF RAIN-STONES IN INNER ASIA

Weather-magic tends to be confined to a certain limited area of Inner Asia. The Yüeh-pan, whom the sources were the first to mention as conjuring up rain and wind in war, lived northwest of the Targhabatai Mountains near the Ili River. According to Islamic tradition, the rain-stone of the Turks is used in the land of the Karluks, in the region of the Western T'ien-shan, or at least originates from there. In Yāqūt's story the Sāmānid ruler, Ismāʿīl ibn Aḥmad faces against the Turkic weather-magicians on his campaign presumably against Talas, the Karluk capital. Kāshgharī witnessed a rain-making ceremony called *yāt* among the Turkic tribe, Yaghmas, who had their habitat in the western and central parts of the T'ien-shan. Finally, the Khwārazmshāh ʿAlāʾ al-Dīn Muḥammad's campaign against the Karakhanids can be traced to the same area. Thus, all these occurrences of weather-magic of the kind named *yād* in Old Turkic and used in warfare can be located in the region of the western and central T'ien-shan (see *Map 1*). Weather-magic was also practised for military purposes outside this territory, to mention the Uighurs only. Still, the western and central parts of the T'ien-shan seem to be the center of this special use of weather-magic. The linguistic analysis of the Turkic gloss *cδyʾ* in the *P 3* Sogdian text also allows one to suppose that the Karluks, who had moved there from their earlier habitat in the east, adopted this local tradition.

The belief that weather-magic can be employed as a "meteorological weapon" can be traced back to the fifth century, when the Yüeh-pan conjured up bad weather against the Juan-juan. Though the ethnicity of the Yüeh-pan cannot be ascertained, the valleys of the T'ien-shan were inhabited by eastern Iranian Saka tribes. It has been argued (see Chapter 3) that *yād*, the Old Turkic word for 'weather-magic', is a loan from an Eastern Middle Iranian language. It is possible that Turkic *yād* was borrowed from Saka with the meaning 'a special kind of weather-magic performed by means of rain-stones and used in warfare'. For while the use of stones in weather-magic is a general, worldwide phenomenon, their use for military purposes is peculiar to Inner Asia. Ultimately, the idea may have been of Iranian origin, though Indo-Iranian *yātuka-* did not mean 'weather-magic'.

As *ǰada*, an Old Turkic loan word in Mongolian makes probable, weather-magic performed by means of stones and used for military purposes was adopted by the Mongols from the Turks. It seems to be too much of a coincidence that in the *Secret History of the Mongols* the Naimans of Turkic origin use weather-magic against the Mongols in the Battle of Köiten, and again it is a Turkic Kangli in the Mongol army who do the same against the Jürchen in 1232.

The beliefs and practices of the early Mongols were different. Boyle[358] rightly remarks that had the Kitans made use of the rain-stone, the Dynastic History of the Liao would hardly have failed to mention the fact. Kitan weather-magic was different, and it served quite peaceful purposes. There is no evidence concerning the nature of Mongol weather-magic prior to the thirteenth century. In any case, we know that the use of bezoars in weather-magic is a Mongol invention. After the Mongol conquest, the military use of the bezoar—called *yada* in Middle Turkic—spread over large territories as a more advanced technique of warfare. Mongol influence on the rain-making beliefs and practices of the Turks can be seen as an improvement in nomadic warfare, an assumption

---

358 1972, p. 190.

that fits very well into our general picture of the Mongols' influence on their neighbours and subjects.

The events described by the sources have so far been analyzed on the level of beliefs. Of course, the practices we have been discussing did not influence the weather in any way. However, we need to consider at this point how weather-magic actually worked, if it worked at all in armed conflicts. The sources report a high success rate, though in the case of the Battle of Köiten, the storm worked against the Naimans who had conjured it up. In Ismāʿīl ibn Aḥmad's story, the Sāmānid ruler himself was believed to have sent the storm back against the Turks with the help of Allah. How weather-magic worked in reality can, perhaps, be best understood by referring to a Western Mongol belief. The Dörböts believe that their neighbours, the Uriankhais, have rain-stones and know how to use them. This is why bad weather is guaranteed whenever the Uriankhais come to plunder the land of the Dörböts. In fact, the Dörböt belief confuses cause and effect. The bad weather, of course, is not a consequence of the weather-magic worked by the Uriankhais. On the contrary, the Uriankhai raid is a consequence of the bad weather: the Uriankhais come to plunder the land of the Dörböts whenever the weather is bad enough to allow them to rustle the horses of the Dörböts undisturbed under the cover of rain, snow and storm.

The way weather-magic worked in warfare can perhaps be explained in a similar way. Nomadic tactics behind the belief consisted in attacking the enemy unexpectedly under the cover of a storm, or charging the troops of the enemy right after they had been weakened by bad weather. The Turks and Mongols had to survive the storm that they believed themselves to have conjured up in better shape than their enemies. Rashīd al-Dīn's account of such a situation is very clear. Tolui Khan, commander of the Mongol troops, ordered his whole army to put on raincoats over their winter clothes and not to dismount from their horses when he ordered the Kangli weather-magician to begin to practice his art against the Jürchens. It is also known from the wider context of the event that the Mongols had taken shelter against the excessive cold, rain, snow and wind in abandoned villages, and even their horses were brought into the houses, while the Jürchen army was compelled to spend three days in the open field. When the Jürchens were sufficiently weakened by the storm, they were effectively assaulted by Tolui's army. We might also add that it was not only men who were adversely affected by the cold and the humidity: weapons were, too. Bows in particular became unusable. The *Chiu T'ang shu* clearly states that all the bows and arrows of the Tibetans struck by the wind and snow were useless, and thus they were easily defeated by the allied Uighur and Chinese forces.

In summation, the varied history of one of the several uses of weather-magic in nomadic warfare can be traced back through the centuries. It first appears in the fifth century among the presumably Eastern Saka tribes in the central and western T'ien-shan; then it was adopted by the Turks, who transmitted the belief in the "meteorological weapon" to the Mongols. The Mongols improved the technique of producing bad weather by introducing the use of bezoars in the ceremony, and the practice and belief were transmitted by the Mongols as a part of nomadic warfare to vast territories of Inner Asia and the Middle East, as shown by the geographical distribution of the Mongol word *ǰada* as a loan word (see *Map 4*). However, the earlier Turkic beliefs and practices also survived, mostly in the western parts of Inner Asia. The belief that weather can be changed and can be used in warfare was current at least until the end of the fifteenth century, and is still a current belief in parts of Inner Asia.

WEATHER-MAGIC AND ITS PRACTITIONERS IN SOCIETY

Weather affects the life of everyone, hence the belief that if it is changed in some way, it will influence the comportment of the whole community. Still, there exists a type of weather-magic among the Turkic and Mongol peoples of recent times that may be considered a kind of private weather-magic, meant to exert its influence over a rather limited time and in a rather limited space. The effects of the magic concern only the persons who performed the rite, and those who made use of the magician's services. Private weather-magic is peculiar to some Turkic and Mongol tribes living in Southern Siberia and Turkestan. For example, the Dörböts think that the Uriankhais freeze rivers if they want to cross them, or can produce snow when they want to track animals. The Mongol Oirots call up cool breezes when they prepare for a long journey. Similarly, the Eastern Turkis and Siberian Turkic tribes, like the Altai Turks, the Tuvins and the Yakuts make use of private weather-magic for much the same purposes. Such magic seems to be due to Mongol influence on the Turks of Turkestan and Southern Siberia, for we find remarkable similarities between the Mongol and Turkic rites and their functions. Furthermore, both Alt. *d'ada*, Yakut *sata*, and ETurki *yada* are Mongol loan words. Among these Mongol and Turkic peoples—including the Yakuts as well—private weather-magic does not require professional help; anyone can do it.

In most cases, however, weather-magic is performed on behalf of a larger community, and both the historical records and the recent descriptions abound in examples of public weather-magic. The weather-magician can be defined by three negative statements.

1. He is not a king. There is no trace in the sources of any weather-magician having had any secular power. He did not become king in the Old Turkic nomadic empires, nor, conversely, is there any information on Old Turkic rulers actively taking part in weather-magic ceremonies.

2. He is not a priest. Among Islamized Turkic peoples, weather-magic rites may be performed by Muslim religious like the Turkish and

Türkmen *imam* and *mulla*, the Bashkir *molla*, the Uzbek Naqshbandi darvishes, and the Eastern Turki *aχun* and *mulla*. Similarly, weather-magic is done by the lamas among the Lamaist Kalmucks and Ordos Mongols. These activities of the Islamic and Lamaist clergy, however, are secondary, and have been adopted from pre-Islamic or pre-Lamaist ceremonies.

3. He is not a shaman. Some authors, like Boyle[359], do consider the weather-magician to be a shaman. However, this view is a consequence of a very widely, or rather vaguely, defined concept of shamanism. Dankoff[360], aware of this difficulty, tentatively considers the Old Turkic *yādčï* to be a special type of *qām* 'diviner'. If, however, the shaman is defined as a social functionary who attains ecstasy by means of the auxiliary spirits, and who through his ecstasy mediates between men and the supernatural world, and who is a healer and a diviner[361], then the weather-magician is not a shaman. On the other hand, the weather-magician's tasks are occasionally undertaken by the shamans; among the Kirghiz, for example, the weather-magician's (*ǰayčï*) duties are sometimes performed by the *bakšï* 'shaman'.

Because of the paucity of sources, many aspects of the activities of weather-magicians are practically unknown. We do not know, for instance, how they were recruited, how they came by their art. What seems certain is that weather-magicians have always been men.

Weather-magicians have been closely associated in their physical person with their art. According to the beliefs of the Kirghiz, the *ǰayčï*'s death is followed by heavy rainfalls that can be stopped only if his corpse is slashed, and his eyebrows and lashes are torn out and burned. There is a vague reference in Kāshgharī to the effect that the *yadčï* may have been paid for his services. The Eastern Turki *yadači* is well paid, provided he is successful in his art.

There are many more examples, however, showing that the weather-magician is more likely to have to make sacrifices to acquire and be able

359 1972, p. 184.
360 1975, p. 77.
361 Hultkrantz 1973, p. 34.

to practice his art. In order to obtain the rain-stone, the Altai Turkic *d'adačï* sacrifices all his fortune, and sells his livestock. Reduced to poverty, he is unable to provide for a family. The Khwārazmian weather-magician in ʿAlāʾ al-Dīn Muḥammad's army complained that whenever he performed the rain-making ceremony, he had misgivings that he might lose a member of his family, or his goods.

If the weather-magician failed to practice his art successfully, he had to face severe sanctions. The unsuccessful Eastern Turki *yadačï* of today still receive "their just deserts", but weather-magicians have also been known to have been whipped or flogged to death for having produced too much rain. In the Empire of the Khwārazmshāhs, two weather-magicians were caught practicing their art and bringing down rain unfavourable for the Khwārazmshāh and his army preparing for a military campaign. On orders of the ruler, the two were wrapped into black felt and buried alive; this way of killing them being considered the most efficient way of counteracting the effects of their magic. This account is of special importance. First, it reveals that as late as the thirteenth century a special kind of human sacrifice was practised by the Turks to ensure the success of a military campaign. Secondly, it shows that the weather-magician could well pay with his life for practicing his art in a way that failed to please. Thirdly, we see felt being used in a curious way. In the *P 3* Sogdian text, frogs were wrapped in black felt and buried, but in that case the rite aimed at producing rain. Perhaps the idea of wrapping the rain-makers into felt was transferred to the weather-magicians from rain-stones. The origin of this rite was the wrapping of rain-stones into felt to prevent their knocking or rubbing against each other. The quoted passage of the *Shāhnāma* (see Chapter 1) reflects the same concept: if the weather-magician is annihilated, the effects of his art cease. In the latter account, the storm stops when the Turkic magicians's hand is cut off by an Iranian hero.

The unauthorized use of weather-magic was thought to cause serious harm. According to the beliefs of the Kirghiz, a lost rain-stone found by a person other than its owner was likely to cause poverty, illness and death. The Bashkirs believe that if someone accidentally touches the rain-stone, he may unwittingly raise a storm. Among the Altai Turks, there exists a belief about children who break the *d'ada-taš* into pieces in a cave, and in this way bring on rain or snow.

When deemed necessary, the weather-magician was called upon to appear, and his services were made use of. As the effects of his magic were of consequence to the whole community, in a great many sources it is the sovereign or some local ruler who orders him to practice his art. Such a case is described by Kāshgharī: *beg yatlattï* "The amīr ordered weather-magic to be performed". Weather-magic as a weapon naturally implied that it was ordered by the commander of the army. The weather-magician seems to be an integral part of the army on a campaign. His presence is attested in the armies of the Uighurs, the Karluks, the Khwārazmshāhs, the Uzbeks and of the Mongols.

In summation, it can be postulated that there existed an official weather-magician (called *yādčï* in Old Turkic) in Turkic societies, one who was believed to have the ability to change the weather by means of dark-coloured horses and rain-stones, and who practised his art at the command of the sovereign. We might add that there were also other sorts of rain-making beliefs and practices.

Owing to his ability to use the "meteorological weapon", the weather-magician had a unique relationship to secular power. He is not supposed to act on his own behalf but only as an executer of orders. The sovereign, though he himself did not take part in weather-magic ceremonies, was the one to decide when they would be held. Tīfāshī, for example, tells us that the Khārazmshāh Jalāl al-Dīn personally supervised the rain-making ceremony performed at his command at Valasjird in 1229. The rain-stones were kept in the treasury of the Khwārazmshahs, and a special office of the "keeper of the rain-stone" was instituted. These customs of the Khwārazmshāhs may shed light on Tamīm ibn Baḥr's account of the rain-stones in the possession of the Toghuzoghuz kings. In Turkic nomadic empires, the possession of rain-stones implied the ability to use them in warfare, and, by extension, the ability to use the "meteorological weapon" implied the possession of power.

APPENDIX: ALTTÜRKISCHE FRAGMENTE ÜBER DEN REGENSTEIN

VON P. ZIEME

Aus bisher publizierten alttürkischen Texten sind *yadčï* "Regenhervorbringer" oder allgemeiner "Zauberer" (*U II* 84_{12}, *TT IV* A 60; vgl. Clauson 1972, 886b) sowie die Verbindung *yat yatlan-* "to perform magical ceremonies" (Clauson 1972, 981a) in *TT X* 387 (in der dazugehörigen Anm. findet man die weiteren Belege für diese Junktur) bekannt. Für die richtige Interpretation wichtig erscheint mir der Beleg in *TT X 561* f.: *yat yatlan-γučï bramn* "der magische Zeremonien verrichtend Brahmane". Während K. Röhrborn (1977 ff. 145 a) dieser Deutung noch kritisch gegenüberstand, übersetzt er jetzt in seiner Edition von *Xuanzang VII* (Röhrborn 1991, 1110) *[yat] yatlanγu sïruq̈-lar* durch "Stab[figuren], um die Regenstein [zeremonie] auszuführen." (*[yat] yatlanγu* ist gegenüber dem chin. Text Takakusu et al. 1924-35, 2053, Vol. L, S. 259 c 2 eine erklärende, verdeutlichende Zugabe).

Das bereits aus diesen Belegen deutlich werdende Nebeneinander von *yad* und *yat* setzt sich in den folgenden Stellen aus noch unpublizierten Texten fort.

1. In einem Text über den Wettstreit zwischen Śāriputra und Raudrāksa (vgl. meine in Vorbereitung befindliche Arbeit *Buddhistische Magie in alttürkischem Gewande*) heißt es (Z. 22): *bälgürḍmäk tägšürmäk üzä yad qïlalïm biz blgürḍäli [m]* "Durch Hervorbringungen und Verwandlungen wollen wir Zauber machen, wollen wir hervorbringen." Dieser Wortlaut entspricht grosso modo dem Chinesischen 我現神通 *wo xian shen tong* "wir manifestieren außergewöhnliche Kräfte" (eds. Takakasu et al. 1924-35, 191, Vol. III, S. 968 a 7).

2. Das aus Sängim stammende Fragment *T II S 501 (U 3004)* der Berliner Turfansammlung könnte Teil eines buddhistisch-tantrischen Werkes gewesen sein (die Identifizierung steht noch aus):

(recto?)

1 [ ]lïγ ïrγaqïn [ä]mgäk[ ]
2 [ ] ornïntïn adïrïp [ ]mïš buyanïn
3 [äviri]p : ärkimin iltip tapïmïn išlät
4 [-ip] ymä yad tašlarïn sürtüp yavlaq aγu
5 [ ]γup özlüglärig ölürüp : q̈or γat

(verso?)

1 [ ]ïγïn adruq adruq alïn altaγïn
2 [ ] mantal bap aγ̈ïr qarγïš-lγ arvïš-larïγ
3 [ ] q̈ayu včir sala ïnča ärklig ögrünčü
4 [ ] bavanïnta divi[ ]l[ ]r oot
5 [ ] ört yaγ[ ]an [ ]

Es folge eine vorläufige Übersetzung:

(recto?) (...) mit dem (...)-Haken (...) [L]eid(...) vom Ort des [...] getrennt, die [...] Verdienste (*puṇya*) zugewendet, meine Kraft fortgeführt, meinen Wunsch ausgeführt habend [...], auch die Regensteine gerieben, starke Gifte [...], Lebewesen getötet habend, Schaden (...)

(verso?) (...) mit verschiedenen Mitteln und Methoden [...] ein Mandala gebunden habend, schwere Fluch-Dhāraṇīs [...] welchen Vajra schwingend, so mächtige Freude [...] im Palast des [...] Feuer [...] Flamme (...)

3. Ein im Museum für Indische Kunst, Berlin aufbewahrtes Fragment (*MIK III 192*) hat auf seiner Rückseite den folgenden Text in uigurischer Kursivschrift:

1 [ ]l[ ] b[o]l[ ]
2 [ ] yad yadlayïn tisär ät'özin
3 [ ]γ küzädm[iš krgäk] . ät'özin küzädmäsär uluγ
4 ada-qa tušar . ät'özin biläsär idi yaraγu ärmäz

5 [ ] yadčï är tašïγ otuγ učuz tutγu ärmäz . ko̤ngül
6 [ ]g tutmïš krgäk . yad tašïn bir ay üč
7 [qata] [ät]'özin yumïš krgäk . qra küž̤i taγ ärdini uruγi käkü[ ]
8 [ ] bo[ ] üzä išlämiš krgäk . bir [ ]
9 [ ] ärür [ ]
10 [ ]n [ ]
11 [ ] ko̤[ ]
12 [ ]an [ ]

Vorläufig möchte ich diesen Text wie folgt übersetzen:

(...) wenn man die Regenstein(zeremonie) durchführen will, [muß man den Regenstein] selbst behüten. Wenn man [ihn] nicht behütet, gerät man in große Gefahr. Wenn man [ihn] selbst..., ist es ganz und gar nicht passend. Der Regensteinzauberer darf den Stein und das Feuer nicht für gering halten. [Den] Sinn muß man [...] halten. Den Regenstein muß [der Regensteinzauberer] selbst in einem Monat drei[mal] waschen. Schwarzer Weihrauch, Bergjuwel (?) ..., ..., mit diesen [...] muß man es bewerkstelligen. (...)

4. In einem Lobpreis der militärischen Tüchtigkeit eines uigurischen Bäg aus Qočo (*T II D 96* [*Ch/U 3916*], (vgl. Zieme 1989, S. 447) steht folgender Vers:

at arqasïnda atlamaq
yanga boyunta yatlamaq

(korrekter ist die Variente in einem Passus über die Fähigkeiten eines *kṣatrika*-Prinzen, *T II T 1183* [*Ch/U 6091*] verso 6:

at arqasïnda atlamaq
yanga boyun-ïnta yadlamaq

Während ich zunächst für *yatlamaq* von *yat* "fremd" ausgegangen bin und obige Stelle durch

> auf dem Pferderücken reiten,
> auf dem Elefantennacken Fremde attackieren

übersetzt habe, halte ich es jetzt für wahrscheinlicher, in *yadlamaq/yatlamaq* eine Ableitung des obigen *yad* zu sehen, so daß wie folgt zu übersetzen wäre:

> auf dem Pferderücken reiten,
> auf dem Elefentennacken zaubern.

In der indischen Kultur, und auf diese sind Wendungen wie die besprochene letztendlich zurückzuführen, hat der Elefant eine Beziehung zur Magie. H. Zimmer (1979, S. 46) schreibt: "Ihre Kraft als magische Regenerwirker steht ihrem Wert als Reittiere des Königs und als stärkste Waffengattung in Schlachten voran."

Aus den hier zusammengestellten Texten läßt sich zeigen, daß die magische Regenwirkung durch Praktiken mit einem Regenstein bei den Uiguren in der Turfan-Oase bekannt waren. Entsprechende Wendungen dienten offenbar auch, um magische Handlungen allgemein auszudrücken. Dies geht vor allem aus dem unter 1 zitierten Text hervor, für den allein es gelungen ist, eine chinisische Parallele zu finden.

Übersicht über die hier nachgewiesenen Wendungen mit *yad*:

yad qïl-
yad yadla-
yat yatlan-
yat yatlanγučï bramn

yatlamaq
yadlamaq
yadčï
yadčï är
yad tašlarïn sürt-
yad tašïn (...) yu-

BIBLIOGRAPHY

ABBREVIATIONS

AÜDTCFD	*Ankara Üniversitesi Dil ve Tarih-Coğrafya Fakültesi Dergisi*
ADAW	*Abhandlungen der Deutschen Akademie der Wissenschaften*
AEMA	*Archivum Eurasiae Medii Aevi*
AKPAW	*Abhandlungen der Königlichen Preussischen Akademie der Wissenschaften*
AM	*Asia Major*
AOH	*Acta Orientalia Academiae Scientiarum Hungaricae*
AzRS 1985	*See Azizbekov 1985*
BEFEO	*Bulletin de l'Ecole Française d'Extrême-Orient*
BRS 1958	See Akhmerov et al. 1958
BSOAS	*Bulletin of the School of Oriental and African Studies*
CAJ	*Central Asiatic Journal*
EI	*The Encylopaedia of Islam.* New Edition (Leiden)
GagRMS 1973	See Baskakov at al. 1973
IIJ	*Indo-Iranian Journal*
IÜEFTED	*Istanbul Üniversitesi Edebiyat Fakültesi Tarih Enstitüsü Dergisi*
JA	*Journal Asiatique*
JAOS	*Journal of the American Oriental Society*
JRAS	*Journal of the Royal Asiatic Society of Great Britain and Ireland*
JSFOu	*Journal de la Société Finno-Ougrienne*
KarRPS 1974	See Baskakov et al. 1974
MSFOu	*Mémoires de la Société Finno-Ougrienne*
RHR	*Revue de l'Histoire des Religions*
SÉ	*Sovetskaya étnografiya*
SKPAW	*Sitzungsberichte der Königlichen Preussischen Akademie der Wissenschaften*
SMAÉ	*Sbornik muzeya antropologii i étnografii*
SPAW	*Sitzungsberichte der Preussischen Akademie der Wissenschaften*
TadRS 1954	See Rakhimi—Uspeskaya 1954
TP	*T'oung Pao*
TPS	*Transactions of the Philological Society*
TrkmRS 1968	See Baskakov et al. 1968
TuvRS 1968	See Tenishev 1968

ZDMG Zeitschrift der Deutschen Morgenländischen Gesellschaft

Aalto, P. (1971), "Iranian Contacts of the Turks in Pre-Islamic Times," in L. Ligeti (ed.), *Studia Turcica*. Budapest, pp. 29—37 (Bibliotheca Orientalis Hungarica XVII)

Abramzon, S.M. (1971), *Kirgizï i ikh étnogeneticheskie i istoriko-kul'turnïe svyazi*. Leningrad (Akademiya Nauk SSSR. Institut Étnografii im. N.N. Miklukho-Maklaya)

(1978), "Étnograficheskie issledovaniya S.E. Malova," in *Tyurkologicheskiy sbornik 1975* (Moskva), pp. 12—25.

Acıpayamlı, O. (1963—64), "Türkiye'de yağmur duası," *AÜDTCFD* XXI pp. 1—39, XXII pp. 221—50.

Akhmerov, K.Z. et al. (1958) (ed.), *Bashkirsko-russkiy slovar'*. Moskva.

Alekseev, N.A. (1980), *Rannie formï religii tyurkoyazychnïkh narodov Sibirii*. Novosobirsk.

Ali-zade, A.A. (ed.) (1980), Faḍlallāh Rashīd ad-Dīn, *Dzhāmi' at-tavārīkh*. Tom. II. Chast' 1. Moskva.

Andrian, F.F. von, (1893), "Ueber den Wetterzauber der Altaier," *Correpondenz-Blatt der Deutschen Gesellschaft für Anthropologie, Ethnology und Urgeschichte* XXIV Nr. 8, pp. 57—68.

Ashmarin, N.I. (1928—50), *Thesaurus linguae Tschuvaschorum*, 17 vols. Cheboksarï.

Azizbekov, Kh.A. (1985) (ed.), *Azerbaydzhansko—russkiy slovar'*. Baku.

Bahār, M. (ed.) (1318/1939), *Mujmal al-Tawārīkh*. Tehran.

Bailey, H.W. (1979), *Dictionary of Khotan Saka*. Cambridge—London—New York—Melbourne.

Bang, W. (1915), "Zur Kritik und Erklärung der Berliner Uigurischen Turfanfragmente," *SKPAW* 39, pp. 623—35.

Bang, W.—A.von Gabain (1930), "Türkische Turfan-Texte. IV," *SPAW* XXIV, pp. 1—20.

Barbier de Meynard, A.C. (1886), *Dictionnaire turc-français*, 2 vols. Paris (Publications de l'École des Langues Orientales Vivantes IIe Série, Tomes IV—V)

Barthold, W. (1956—1958), *Four Studies on Central Asia*, 2 vols. Leiden. (1968), *Turkestan Down to the Mongol Invasion*. London ("E.J.W. Gibb Memorial" Series N. S. Vol. V)

Barthold, W.—B. Spuler (1978), "Issik-Kul," In *EI* Vol. IV, pp. 212—13.

Bartholomae, Ch. (1904), *Altiranisches Wörterbuch*. Strassburg.

Başgöz, I. (1967), "Rain-making Ceremonies in Turkey and Seasonal Festivals," *JAOS* 87, pp. 304—6.

Basilov, V.N. (1988) "Yada," in S.A. Tokarev (ed.), *Mifï narodov mira. Éntsiklopediya*, 2 vols (Moskva), Vol. II. p. 681.

Baskakov, N.A. et al. (eds.) (1968), *Turkmensko—russkiy slovar'*. Moskva 1968.

Baskakov, N.A. et al. (eds.) (1973), *Gagauzsko—russko—moldavskiy slovar'*. Moskva.

Baskakov, N.A. et al. (eds.) (1974), *Karaimsko—russko—pol'skiy slovar'*. Moskva.

Bawden, C.R. (1955), *The Mongol Chronicle Altan Tobči*. Wiesbaden (Göttinger Asiatische Forschungen, Band 5)

Bayalieva, T.D. (1972), *Doislamskie verovaniya i ikh perezhitki u kirgizov*. Frunze (Akademiya nauk Kirgizskoy SSR. Institut Istorii)

Benveniste, E. (1940), *Textes Sogdiens*. Paris (Mission Pelliot en Asie Centrale. Serie in-quarto III)

Berezin, I.N. (1858—1861—1868), *Sbornik letopisey. Istoriya mongolov* ... (Trudï vostochnogo otdeleniya imperatorskago arkheologicheskago obshchestva, Vols. 5, 7 and 13)

Bergmann, B. (1804), *Nomadische Streifereien unter den Kalmüken*, 4 vols. Riga.

Beveridge, A.S. (1905), *Babur-name (Memoirs of Babur)*. London ("E.J.W. Gibb Memorial" Series Vol. I)

Bichurin, N.Ya. (1950—53), *Sobranie svedeniy o narodakh obitavshikh v Sredney Azii v drevnie vremena*, 3 vols Moskva—Leningrad (Akademiya nauk SSSR, Institut étnografii imeni N. N. Miklukho-Maklaya)

Bivar, A.D. (1985), "A Persian Fairyland," in *Papers in Honour of Professor Mary Boyce*. Leiden, pp. 25—42 (Acta Iranica. Hommages et Opera Minora Vol. XI)

Bloomfield, M. (1896), "On the Frog-hymn, Rig Veda, vii, 103," *JAOS* 17, pp. 173—9.

Boilot, D.J. (1960), "al-Bīrūnī," in *EI* Vol. I, pp. 1236—8.

Boratav, P.N. (1952), "Istiska," in *Islam Ansiklopedisi* (Istanbul) Vol. XVIII, cc. 1221—4.

(1978), "Rain-making ceremonies among the Turks," in *EI* Vol. IV, c. 271.

Borovkov, A.K. (ed.) (1959), *Uzbeksko-russkiy slovar'*. Moskva.

(1963), *Leksika sredneaziatskogo Tefsira XIII—XIV vv.* Moskva.

Bosworth, C.E. (1978), "K̲h̲^{w}ārazm-shāhs," in *EI* Vol. IV, c. 1O65—8.

(1978a), "Ḳanghli," in *EI* Vol. IV, p. 542.

(1978b), "Ḳarluḳ," in *EI* Vol. IV, pp. 658—9.

Boyce, M. (1975), *A History of Zoroastrianism. Vol. One. The Early Period.* Leiden/Köln (Handbuch der Orientalistik Erste Abt. VIII. Band, 1. Abschnitt, Lief. 2)

Boyle, J.A. (1958), 'Ala-ad-Din 'Ata-Malik Juvaini, *The History of the World-Conqueror* 2 vols. Manchester.

(1971), *The Successors of Genghis Khan*. New York and London.

(1972) "Turkish and Mongolian Shamanism in the Middle Ages," *Folklore* 83, pp. 177—93.

Brockelmann, C. (1925), "Volkskundliches aus Altturkestan," *AM* 2, pp. 110—24.

Budagov, L. (1869—71), *Sravnitel'nïy slovar' turetsko—tatarskikh narechiy so vklyucheniem upotrebitel'neyshikh slov arabskikh i persidskikh i s perevodom na russkiy yazïk*. Sanktpeterburg.

Cheremisov, K.M. (ed.) (1973), *Buryatsko-russkiy slovar'*. Moskva.

Clauson, G. (1960), *Sanglakh. A Persian Guide to the Turkish Language by Muhammad Mahdī Xān*. London ("E.J.W. Gibb Memorial" Series, N. S. XX)

(1962), *Turkish and Mongolian Studies*. London (Prize Publication Fund Vol. XX)

(1972), *An Etymological Dictionary of Pre-Thirteenth-Century Turkish*. Oxford.

Czeglédy, K. (1973), "Gardizi on the History of Central Asia," *AOH* XXVII, pp. 257—67.

(1983), "From East to West: The Age of Nomadic Migrations in Eurasia," *AEMA* III, pp. 25—125 (Transl. from Hungarian by P.B. Golden)

Dankoff, R. (1975), "Kāšġarī on the Beliefs and Superstitions of the Turks," *JAOS* 95, pp. 68—80.

Dankoff, R.—J. Kelly (1982-85), *Maḥmūd al-Kāšγarī, Compendium of the Turkic Dialects*, 3 vols. Cambridge Mass.

Demidov, S. (1964), "On Religious Syncretism Among the Turkmens in the XIX and the Beginning of the XX Centuries," in *VII International Congress of Anthropological and Ethnological Sciences* (Moscow 1964), pp. 1—13.

[Türkiye'de Halk Ağzından] Derleme Sözlüğü, 12 vols. (Ankara) 1963—82 (Türk Dil Kurumu Yayınları — Sayı 211/1—12).

Desmaisons, J.J.R. (1908—14), *Dictionnaire persan—français*, 4 vols. Rome.

Desmaisons, Le Baron (1871—74), *Histoire des Mongols et des Tatares*, 2 vols. St. Pétersbourg.

Dingel'shtedt, N. (1893), *Opït izucheniya irrigatsii Turkestanskago kraya. Sïr-dar'inskaya oblast'*. SPb.

Dodge, B. (1970), *The Fihrist of al-Nadīm. A Tenth-Century Survey of Muslim Culture*, 2 vols. New York—London.

Doerfer, G. (1963—75), *Türkische und mongolische Elemente im Neupersischen. Band I: Mongolische Elemente im Neupersischen (1963). Band II: Türkische Elemente im Neupersischen alif bis tā (1965); Band III: ǧīm bis kāf (1967); Band IV: Türkische Elemente im Neupersischen (Schluss) und Register zur Gesemtarbeit (1975).* Wiesbaden.

Dresden, M. (1983), "Sogdian Language and Literature," in E. Yarshater (ed.), *The Cambridge History of Iran* Vol. 3/1—2. *The Seleucid, Parthian and Sasanian Periods* (Cambridge), pp. 1216—29.

Ecsedy, I. (1980), "A Contribution to the History of Karluks in the T'ang Period," *AOH* XXXIV, pp. 23—37.

Elias, N. (ed.)—E.D. Ross (transl.) (1895), *The Tarikh-i Rashidi of Mirza Muhammad Haidar, Dughlát A History of the Moghuls of Central Asia*. London.

Fahd, T. (1966), "Le monde du sorcier en Islam," in *Le monde du sorcier* (Paris) pp. 155—204 (Sources Orientales, Vol. VII)

(1978) "Istisḳā," in *EI* Vol. IV, pp. 269—70.

Franke, H. (1956), *Beiträge zur Kulturgeschichte Chinas unter der Mongolenherrschaft. Das* Shan-kü sin-hua *des Yang Yü*. Wiesbaden (Abhandlungen für die Kunde des Morgenlandes XXXII,2)

(1990), "The forest peoples of Manchuria: Kitans and Jurchens," in D. Sinor (ed.), *The Cambridge History of Early Inner Asia* (Cambridge), pp. 400—23.

Frazer, J.G. (1911), *The Golden Bough. A Study in Magic and Religion. Part I. The Magic Art and the Evolution of Kings*, 2 vols. London.

Gabain, A. von (1959), *Türkische Turfantexte X. Das Avadāna des Dämons Ātavaka*. Berlin (ADAW. Klasse für Sprachen, Literatur und Kunst. 1958, Nr. 1)

Gabrieli, F. (1971), "Ibn Muḳaffa'," in *EI* Vol. III, pp. 883—5.

Gershevitch, I. (1954), *A Grammar of Manichean Sogdian*. Oxford (Publications of the Philological Society)

Gertsenberg, L.G. (1981), *Khotanosakskiy yazïk* in V.I. Abaev et al. (eds.), *Osnovï iranskogo yazïkoznaniya. Sredneiranskie yazïki*. Moskva, pp. 233—313.

Gharib, B. (1969), "Telesm-e bārān az yak matn-e soġdi (Rain Talisman)," *Nashriyat-e Anjoman-e Farhang-e Irân-e Bâstân (The Ancient Iranian Cultural Society Bulletin)* Vol. VII. No. 1, pp. 12—24.

Goeje, M.J. de (1885), Ibn al-Faḳih, *Compendium libri Kitāb al-Boldān*. (Bibliotheca Geographorum Arabicorum Vol. V)

Golden, P. (1972), "The Migrations of the Oğuz," *Archivum Ottomanicum* IV, pp. 45—84.

(1990), "The Karakhanids and early Islam," in (ed.) D. Sinor, *The Cambridge History of Early Inner Asia* (Cambridge), pp. 343—70.

Gordlevskiy, V.A. (1934) "Bakha-ud-din Nakshbend bukharskiy (k voprosu o nasloeniyakh v Islame)," in (ed.) Yu. Krachkovskiy, *Sergeyu Fedorovichu Ol'denburgu k pyatidesyatiletiyu nauchno-obshchestvennoy deyatel'nosti 1882—1932* (Moskva), pp. 147—69.

Grenard, F. (1898), *Le Turkestan et le Tibet*. Paris (J.-L. Dutreuil de Rhins, Mission scientifique La Haute Asie 1890-1895, Vol. II)

Grousset, R. (1970), *The Empire of the Steppes. A History of Central Asia*. New Brunswick, New Jersey (Transl. from the French by N. Walford)

Guidi, I. (1903), *Chronica minora. Pars prior*. Paris.

Ḥabibi, 'Abdo'l Ḥeiy (1968), Gardizi, *Zainu'l-Axbār*. Tehrān (Enteshārāt-e Bonyād-e Farhang-e Irān 37. Manābe'-e Tārikh va Joghrāfiyā-ye Irān 12)

Haenisch, E. (1948), *Die Geheime Geschichte der Mongolen. Aus einer mongolischen Niederschrift des Jahres 1240 von der Insel Kode'e im Keluren Fluss*. Leipzig[2].

Hammer-Pursgtall. [J.] (1840), *Geschichte der goldenen Horde in Kiptschak, das ist: der Mongolen in Russland*. Pesth.

(1856), (ed.) *Geschichte Wassaf's*. Wien.

Harva, U. (1938), *Die religiösen Vorstellungen der altaischen Völker*. Helsinki.

Henning, W.B. (1940), *Sogdica*. London (James G. Forlong Fund, Vol. XXI)

(1945), "Sogdian Tales," *BSOAS* xi, pp. 465—87.

(1945a), "Two Central Asian Words," *TPS*, pp. 150—162.

(1946), "The Sogdian Texts of Paris," *BSOAS* xi, pp. 713—40.

Houdas, O. (1891—5), *Histoire du sultan Djelal ed-Din Mankobirti. Par Mohammad en-Nasavi*. Paris (Publications l'École des Languages Orientales Vivantes, IIIe Serie, Tomes IX-X)

Huart, C. (1899—1919), al-Muṭahhar, *Bad' wa-t-tārīḫ (Commencement et histoire)*. Paris (Publications de l'École des Languages Orientales Vivantes, IVe Serie, XVI—XVIII, Tomes XXI—XXIII)

Hultkrantz, Å. (1973), "A Definition of Shamanism," *Temenos* 9, pp. 25—37.

Ilminski, N. (1857), *Baber-nameh diagataice ad fidem Codicis Petropolitani*. Cazani.

Inan, A. (1954), *Tarihte ve bugün şamanism. Materyaller ve Araştırmalar*. Ankara.

Izbudak, V. (1936), *El-Idrâk Hâşiyesi*. Istanbul.

Jarring, G. (1946—51), *Materials to the Knowledge of Eastern Turki. Tales, Poetry, Proverbs, Riddles, Ethnological and Historical Texts From the Southern Parts of Eastern Turkestan*, 4 vols, Lund.

(1961) "A Note on Shamanism in Eastern Turkestan," *Ethnos* 1—2, pp. 1—4.

(1964) *An Eastern Turki-English Dialect Dictionary*. Lund.

(1979—80) "Matters of Ethnological Interest in Swedish Missionary Reports From Southern Sinkiang," *Scripta Minora. Regiae Societatis Humaniorum Litterarum Lundensis*, pp. 1—21.

Julien, S. (1847), "Notices sur les pays et les peuples étrangers, tirées des géographies et des annales chinoises, III. Les Ouïgours," *JA* 4. 9, 64, pp. 50—66.

Kałużyński, S. (1961), *Mongolische Elemente in der jakutischen Sprache*. Warszawa.

Kara, G. (1963), "Un glossaire üǰümčin," *AOH* XVI, pp. 1—43.

Keith, A.B. (1917), *Indian Mythology* in *Mythology of All Races*, Vol. VI. Boston.

Khangalov, M.Kh. (1890), "Novïe materialï o shamanstve u buryat," *Zapiski vostochno-sibirskago otdela imperatorskago russkago geograficheskago obshchestva po étnografii*, Tom II, vïp. 1—y Irkutsk.

Khudyakov. I.A. (1969), *Kratkoe opisanie Verkhoyanskoe okruga*. Leningrad.

Kičikov, A.Š. (1985), "Archaische Motive bei der Herkunft des Helden und ihre Umbildungen in den J̌anγar-Versionen," in (ed.) W. Heissig, *Fragen der mongolischen Heldendichtung* Band III. Wiesbaden, pp. 301—72.

Kononov, A.N. (1972), *Istoriya izucheniya tyurkskikh yazïkov v Rossii. Dooktyabr'skiy period*. Leningrad.

Kowalewski, J.É. (1844—49), *Dictionnaire mongol—russe-français*, 3 vols. Kazan.

Köprülü Zadè, M.F. (1925), "Une institution magique chez les anciens Turcs: yat," in *Actes du Congrès International d'Histoire des Religions* (Paris), Tome II, pp. 440—51.

Kraus, P. (1942—43), *Jābir ibn Ḥayyān. Contribution à l'histoire des idées scientifiques dans l'Islam. Vol. I. Le corpus des écrits jābiriens. Vol. II. Jābir et la science grecque.* Le Caire (Mémoires a l'Institut d'Égypte, Vols. 44—45)

Krenkow. S. (ed.) (1936—37), Al-Bīrūnī, *Kitāb al-Jamāhir fī Ma 'rifat al-Jawāhir*. Haidarābād.

Laufer, B. (1919) *Sino—Iranica. Chinese Contributions to the History of Civilization in Ancient Iran*. Chicago.

Lessing, F. (1960), *Mongolian—English Dictionary*. Bloomington.

Levy, R. (1967), *The Epic of the Kings. Shah-Nama, the national epic of Persia by Ferdowsi*. London.

Liu, Mau-Tsai (1958), *Die chinesischen Nachrichten zur Geschichte der Ost-Türken (T'u-küe)*, 2 vols. Wiesbaden (Göttinger Asiatische Forschungen 10)

Logofat, D.H. (1913), *V gorakh i na ravninakh Bukharï (Ocherki Sredney Azii)*. S.-Peterburg.

Luvsandéndév, A. (1957), *Mongol'sko—russkiy slovar'*. Moskva.

MacKenzie, D.N. (1971), *A Concise Pahlavi Dictionary*. London.

Mackerras, C. (1972), *The Uighur Empire According to the T'ang Dynastic Histories. A Study in Sino—Uighur Relations 744—840*. Canberra (Asian Publication Series 2)

Malov, S.É. (1918), "Shamanstvo u sartov Vostochnogo Turkestana," *Sbornik muzeya antropologii i étnografii*, Vol. 5, pp. 1—16.

(1947), "Shamanskiy kamen' 'yada' u tyurkov zapadnogo Kitaya," *SÉ* 1, pp. 151—60.

Malov, S.É. (1957), *Yazïk zhëltïkh uygurov. Slovar' i grammatika*. Alma-Ata.

Malyavkin, A.G. (1974), *Materialï po istorii uygurov v IX—VII. vv. Istoriya kul'tura Vostoka Azii*. Tom II. Novosibirsk.

Marquart, J. (1914), *Über das Volkstum der Komanen* in W. Bang and J. Marquart, *Osttürkische Dialektstudien*. Berlin (Abhandlungen der königlichen Gesellschaft der Wissenschaften zu Göttingen. Philologisch-historische Klasse NF. Bd. XIII. No. 1)

Martinez, A.P. (1982), "Gardīzī's Two Chapters on the Turks," *AEMA* II, pp. 109—217.

Massé, H. (1938), *Croyances et coutumes persanes*, 2 vols. Paris (Les Litteratures Populaires de Toutes les Nations N.S. T. IV)

Minorsky, V. (1937), *Ḥudūd al-'Ālam 'The Regions of the World'. A Persian Geography 372 A.H.—982 A.D.* London.

(1948), "Tamīm ibn Baḥr's Journey to the Uyghurs," *BSOAS* xii, 2, pp. 275—305.

Mir Izzet Ullah (1843), "Travels beyond the Himalaya," *JRAS* VII, 283—342 (Republished from the Calcutta Oriental Quarterly Magazine, 1825)

Mokri, M. (1959), "Les vents du Kurdistan," *JA* 247, pp. 479—97.

Monier-Williams, M. (1899), *A Sanskrit—English Dictionary Etymologically and Philologically Arranged with Special Reference to Cognate Indo-European Languages*. Oxford.

Morgenstierne, G. (1929), *Indo-Iranian Frontier Languages. Vol. I. Parachi and Ormuri*. Oslo.

Mostaert, A. (1968), *Dictionnaire Ordos*², 3 vols. Peking.

(1956), "Matériaux ethnographiques relatifs aux Mongols ordos," *CAJ* II, pp. 241—94.

Munkácsi, B. (1900), "Arische Sprachdenkmäler in türkischen Lehnwörter," *Keleti Szemle* I, pp. 156—8.

Müller, F.W.K. (1910), *Uigurica II* Berlin (APAW Phil.-hist. Cl. 1910)

Nadzhip, É.N. (1968), *Uygursko—russkiy slovar'* Moskva.

Nau, F. (1913), "En Asie Centrale. Textes nestoriens, magiques, mazdéens, bardesanites, marcionites, manichéens, moniens," *JA* 11. 2, pp. 451—63.

Nikiforov, N.Ya. (1915), *Anosskiy sbornik. Sobranie skazok altaytsev s primechaiyami G. N. Potanina.* Omsk.

Nöldeke, Th. (1893), *Die von Guidi herausgegebene syrische Chronik.* Berlin (Sitzungberichte der kaiserlichen Akademie der Wissenschaften. Philosophisch-historische Classe 128)

Ol'denburg, S. (1918), "Kratkie zametki o perikhonakh i dua-khonakh v Kuchare," *SMAÉ* 5, pp. 17—20.

Pallas, P. (1771—76), *Reise durch verschiedene Provinzen des Russischen Reichs*, 4 vols. St. Petersburg.

(1776—1801), *Sammlungen historischer Nachrichten über die mongolischen Völkerschaften*, 2 vols. St. Petersburg.

Pavet de Courteille, A. (1870), *Dictionnaire turc-oriental*. Paris.

Pekarskiy, É.K. (1917-30), *Slovar' yakutskago yazïka*, 3 vols. SPbg.

Pelliot, P. (1903), [Review of] *E. H. Parker, China, the Avars, and the Franks (Asiatic Quarterly Review, avril 1902, pp. 346—360)*: *BEFEO* 3, pp. 99—100.

(1930), "Sur la légende d'Uγuz-khan en écriture ouigoure," *TP* XXVII, pp. 247—358.

(1949), *Notes sur l'histoire de la Horde d'Or. Oeuvres posthumus de Paul Pelliot*. Publiées sous les auspices de l'Académie des Inscriptions et Belles-Lettres et avec le concours du Centre National de la Recherche Scientifique II. Paris.

(1959—1963—1973), *Notes on Marco Polo. Ouvrage posthume*, 3 vols. Paris.

(1960), *Notes critiques d'histoire Kalmouke*. Paris.

Pelliot, P.—L. Hambis (1951), *Histoire des campagnes de Gengis Khan. Cheng-wou ts'in-tcheng lou*. Tome I. Leiden.

Popov, A.A. (1949), "Materialï po istorii religii yakutov v. Viyuyskogo okruga (Predislovie V. G. Bogoraza)," in *SMAÉ AN SSSR. Institut étnografii i. N. N. Miklukho-Maklaya* (Moskva—Leningrad), pp. 255—323.

Poppe, N. (1955), *Introduction to Mongolian Comparative Studies*. Helsinki (*MSFOu* 110)

Poppe, N. (1955a), "The Turkic Loan Words in Middle Mongolian," *CAJ* I, pp. 36—42.

Potanin, G.N. (1881—83), *Ocherki Severo-Zapadnoy Mongolii*, 4 vols. St. Peterburg.

(1893), *Tangutsko-tibetskaya okraina Kitaya i tsentral'naya Mongoliya. Puteshestvie G. N. Potanina 1884—1886*, 2 vols. S.-Peterburg.

(1917), "Kazak-kirgizskaya i altayskiya predaniya, legendï i skazki," *Zhivaya starina* XXV (1916), Petrograd.

Potapov, L.P. (1960), "Materialï po étnografii tuvintsev rayonov Mongun-taygi i Kara-kholya," in L.P. Potapov (ed.), *Trudï tuvinskoy kompleksnoy arkheologo-étnograficheskoy ékspeditsii* Tom 1. *Materialï po arkheologii i étnografii zapadnoy Tuvï* (Moskva—Leningrad), pp. 171—237.

(1978), "K voprosu o drevnetyurkskoy osnove i datirov-ke altayskogo shamanastva," in *Étnografiya narodov Altaya i Zapadnoy Sibiri* (Novosibirsk), pp. 3—36.

(1991), *Altayskiy shamanizm*. Leningrad (Akademiya Nauk SSSR Institut étnografii im. N.N. Miklukho-Maklaya)

Pritsak, O. (1951), "Von den Karluk zu den Karachaniden," *ZDMG* 101, pp. 270—300.

Qazvini, M.M. (1912—1916—1937), *The Ta'ríkh-i-Jahán-Gushá of 'Alá'u'd-Dīn 'tâ-Malik-i-Juwayní*, 3 vols. London ("E.J.W. Gibb Memorial" Series, Old Series Vol. XVI/1, 2, 3)

Quatremère, É. (1836), Raschid-eldin, *Histoire des Mongols de la Perse*. Paris.

Rachewiltz, I. de (1972), *Index To the Secret History of the Mongols*. Bloomington (Indiana University Publications. Uralic and Altaic Series, Vol. 121)

(1974, 1985), "The Secret History of the Mongols," *Papers on Far Eastern History* 10, 1974 September, 31 March 1985.

Radloff, W. (1866), *Die Sprachen der türkischen Stämme Süd-Sibiriens und der Dsungarischen Steppe. I. Abt. Proben der Volksliteratur der türkischen Stämme Süd-Sibiriens und der Dsungarischen Steppe. I. Theil: Die Dialecte des eigentlichen Altai: Der Altaier,*

Teleuten, Lebed-Tataren. Schoren und Sojonen 1. (Texts) 2. Übersetzung. St. Petersburg.

(1870), *Die Sprachen der türkischen Stämme Süd-Sibiriens und der Dsungarischen Steppe. I. Abt. Proben der Volksliteratur der türkischen Stämme Süd-Sibiriens III. Theil. Kirgisischen Mundarten 1. (Texts) 2. Übersetzung*. St. Petersburg.

(1893), *Aus Sibirien. Lose Blätter aus meinem Tagebuche* 2 vols. Leipzig.

(1888—1911), *Versuch eines Wörterbuches der türk-Dialecte* 4 vols. St. Petersburg.

Rakhimi, M.V.—L.V. Uspenskaya (eds.) (1954), *Tadzhiksko—russkiy slovar'*. Moskva.

Ramstedt, G.J. (1935), *Kalmückisches Wörterbuch*. Helsinki (Lexica Societatis Fenno-Ugricae III)

Räsänen, M. (1969—71), *Versuch eines etymologischen Wörterbuchs der Türksprachen I. Wortregister II* (Zusammengestellt v. I. Kecskeméti) Helsinki (Lexica Societatis Fenno-Ugricae XVII, 1—2)

Redhouse, J.W. (1890), *A Turkish and English Lexicon*. Constantinople.

Rehatsek, E. (1891), *The Rauzat-us-safa; or Garden of Purity. Containing The Histories of Prophets, Kings, and Khalifs* by Muhammad bin Khâvendshâh bin Mahmûd, commonly called Mirkhond. Part I. Vol. 1. London (Oriental Translation Fund. New Series I)

Reichelt, H. (1931), *Die soghdischen Handschriftenreste des Briti-schen Museums. II. Theil: Die nicht-buddhistischen Texte*. Heidelberg.

Ritter, H.—M. Plessner (1962), *"Picatrix" Das Ziel des Weisen von Pseudo-Mağrīṭī*. London (Studies of the Warburg Institute 27)

Roemer, H.R. (1986), "The Safavid Period," in P. Jackson (ed.), *The Cambridge History of Iran*. Vol. 6. *The Timurid and Safavid Periods* (Cambridge), pp. 189—35.

Röhrborn, K. (1977 ff.), *Uigurisches Wörterbuch*. Wiesbaden.

(1991), *Die alttürkische Hsüen-tsang-Biographie* VII. Wiesbaden.

Ross, E.D. (1927), *Ta 'rīkh-i Fakhru'd-Dīn Mubárakshâh*. London (James G. Forlong Fund)

Roux, J.-P. (1956—1957) "Tängri. Essai sur le ciel-dieu des peuples altaïques," *RHR* 149, pp. 49—82, 197—230, 150, pp. 27—54, 172—212.

(1958), "Le nom du chaman dans les textes turco—mongols," *Anthropos* 53, pp. 133—42.

(1958a) "Éléments chamaniques dans les textes pré-mongols," *Anthropos* 53, pp. 441—56.

(1984), *La religion des Turcs et des Mongols*. Paris.

Ruska, J. (1913), "Kazwīnīstudien," *Der Islam* 4, pp. 14—66, 236—62.

Sâmi, Š. (1901) *Qāmūs-i Türkī*. [Constantinople].

Schafer, Ch. (1876), *Histoire de l'Asie Centrale par Mir Abdoul Kerim Boukhary*. Paris (Publications l'École des Languages Orientales Vivantes, 1e Série, Tomes I—II)

Schmidt, P.W. (1949), *Der Ursprung der Gottesidee. Band IX. Die asiatischen Hirtenvölker. 3. Abt. Die primären Hirtenvölker der Alt-Türken, der Altai- und der Abakan-Tataren*. Freiburg.

Seroshevskiy, A.I. (1896), *Yakutï*. St. Petersburg.

Şeşen, R. (1981), "Klâsik Islâm kaynaklarına göre eski Türklerin dini ve Şaman kelimesinin menşei (Başlangıçtan Moğol istilâsına kadar)," *IÜEFTED* 10—11, pp. 57—90.

Shnitnikov, B.N. (1966), *Kazakh—English Dictionary*. London—The Hague—Paris (Indiana University Publications. Uralic and Altaic Series, Vol. 28)

Sieroszewski, W. (1902), "Du chamanisme d'après les croyances des Yakoutes," *RHR* 46, pp. 204—33, 299—358.

Sims-Williams, N. (1976), "The Sogdian Fragments of the British Library," *IIJ* XVIII, pp. 43—82.

(1983), "Indian Elements in Parthian and Sogdian," in K. Röhrborn—W. Veenker (hrsg.), *Sprachen des Buddhismus in*

Zentralasien. Vorträge des Hamburger Symposions vom 2. Juli bis 5. Juli 1981 (Wiesbaden) pp. 132—41.

(1983a), "Chotano-Sogdica," *BSOAS* XLVI, Part 1, pp. 40—51.

Sinor, D. (1982), "The Legendary Origin of the Türks," in E.V. Žygas—P. Voorheis (eds.), *Folklorica: Festschrift for Felix J. Oinas* (Bloomington), pp. 223—57 (Indiana University Uralic and Altaic Series, Vol. 141)

(1990) (ed.) *The Cambridge History of Early Inner Asia.* Cambridge.

Sokolova, V.S. (1960), *Bartangskie tekstï i slovar'*. Moskva-Leningrad.

[*Türkiye Halk Ağzından] Söz Derleme Dergisi*, 6 vols. (Istanbul—Ankara) 1939—52.

Stein, A. (1921), *Serindia. Detailed Report of Explorations in Central Asia and Westernmost China*, 5 vols. Oxford.

Steingass, F. (1892), *Persian—English Dictionary*. London.

Takakasu et al.(eds.), (1924—35), *Taishō shinshū daizōkyō*. Tokio.

Tanyu, H. (1968), *Türklerde taşla ilgili inançlar*. Ankara (Ankara Üniversitesi Ilâhiyat Fakultesi Yayınları 81)

[Osmanlıcadan Türkçeye Söz Karşılıkları] Tarama Dergisi 1. Istanbul 1934.

[XIII. Yüzyıldan beri Türkiye Türkçesiyle yazılmış kitaplardan toplanan tanıklariyle] Tarama Sözlüğü, 8 vols. (Ankara 1963—77)

Tenishev, É.R. (ed.), *Tuvinsko—russkiy slovar'*. Moskva.

Terzibaşı, A. (1976), "Irak Türkmenleri Arasında Yağmur Duası Törenleri ve Sosyolojik Değeri," in *I. Uluslararası Türk Folklor Kongresi Bildirileri. IV. Cilt. Gelenek—Görenek ve Inançlar.* Ankara, pp. 305—14 (Kültür Bakanlığı Millî Folklor Araştırma Dairesi Yayınları 21, Seminer, Kongre Bildirileri Dizisi: 6)

Timkowski, G. (1827), *Voyage à Péking à travers la Mongolie en 1820 et 1821*, 2 vols. Paris.

Togan, see also Validov.

Togan, Z.V. (1946), *Umumî Türk Tarihine Giriş. Cild I. En eski devirden 16. asra kadar*. Istanbul.

(1948), "Ibn al-Fakih'in Türklere ait haberleri," *Belleten* 45, pp. 11—6.

Tsoloo, J. (1988), *Dialektologicheskiy slovar' mongol'skogo yazïka II (Oyratskoe narechie)*. Ulaanbaatar (in Khalkha)

Ullmann, M. (1972), *Die Natur- und Geheimwissenschaften im Islam. Handbuch der Orientalistik*, Erste Abteilung, Ergänzungsband VI, 2. Abschnitt. Leiden.

Ünver, A.S. (1953), "Yağmur Taşı Hakkında," *Tarih Dergisi* IV, 7, pp. 77—84.

Validov, A.Z. (1924), "Meshkhedskaya rukopis' Ibnu-l'-Fakiha," *Izvestiya Rossiyskoy Akademii Nauk* VI. Seriya. Tom XVIII, pp. 237—48.

Valikhanov, Ch. (1953), *Izbrannïe proizvedeniya*. Alma-Ata.

Vámbéry, H. (1879), *Die primitive Cultur des turko-tatarischen Volkes*. Leipzig.

(1885), *Das Türkenvolk in seinen ethnologischen und ethnografischen Beziehungen*. Leipzig.

Vefik Paşa, A. (1876), *Lehçe-i Osmani* [Constantinople].

Véliaminov-Zernov, V. de (1869), *Dictionaire djagatai-turk*. St. Petersburg.

Verbitskiy, P.V. (1884), *Slovar' altayskago i aladagskago narechiy tyurkskago yazïka*. Kazan.

(1893), *Altayskie inorodtsï*. Moskva.

Vullers, J.A. (1878—84), *Firdusii liber regum qui inscribitur Schahname*, 3 vols. Lugduni Batavorum.

Wittfogel, K.A.—Fêng, Chia-shêng (1949), *History of Chinese Society Liao (907—1125)*. Philadelphia (Transactions of the American Philosophical Society N.S. — Vol. 36)

Wüstenfeld, F. (1848—49), *Zakarijja B. Muḥammed B. Maḥmud al-Cazwini's Kosmographie*. Göttingen.

Yaltkaya, Ş. (1935), "Ebureyhan'ın bir kitabı," *Türkiyat Mecmuası* V. pp. 1—26.

(1943), "Eski Türk Ananelerinin bazı dinî Müesseselere Tesirleri," in *Ikinci Türk Tarih Kongresi. Istanbul 20-25 Eylül 1937. Kongrenin Çalışmaları, Kongreye Sunulan Tebliğler.* (Istanbul), pp. 690—8 (Türk Tarih Kurumu Yayınlarından IX. Seri: No. 2)

Yāqūt al-Rūmī (1979), *Mu 'djam al-buldān*, 5 vols. Beyrouth.

Yarshater, E. (1983), "Iranian National History," in (ed.) E. Yarshater, *The Cambridge History of Iran, Vol. 3/1—2. The Seleucid, Parthian and Sasanian Periods* (Cambridge), pp. 359—477.

Yule, H. (1921), *The Book of Ser Marco Polo the Venetian Concerning the Kingdoms and Marvels of the East*, 2 vols. London.

Yudakhin, K.K. (1985), *Kirgizsko-russkiy slovar'*[2] Moskva.

Yunusaliev, B.M. (1958), *Manas. Birinči bölük. I. Kitep. Kïskartïlïp biriktirilgen variant*. Frunze.

Zenker, J.Th. (1866), *Türkisch-arabisch-persisches Handwörterbuch*. Leipzig.

Zieme, P. (1989), "Titulaturen und Elogen uigurischer Könige," in K. Sagaster and H. Eimer (eds.) *Religious and Lay Symbolism in the Altaic World and Other Papers*. Wiesbaden. pp. 443—450.

Zimmer, H. (1979), *Spiel um den Elefanten. Ein Buch von indischer Natur*. Suhrkamp.

Zimonyi, I. (1990), *The Origins of the Volga Bulghars*. Szeged (Studia Uralo-Altaica 32)

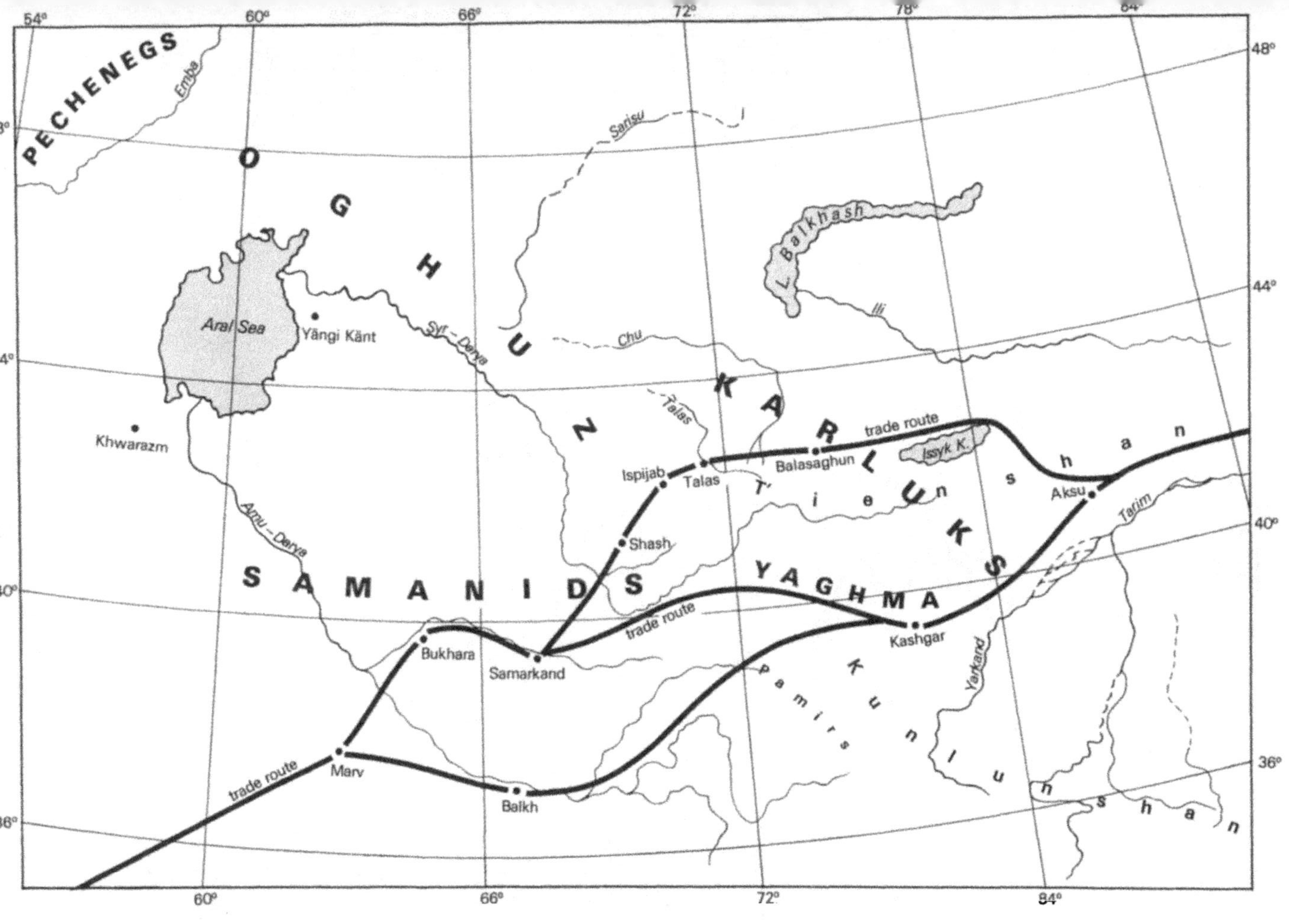

Map 1. : Western Inner Asia in the 9th century

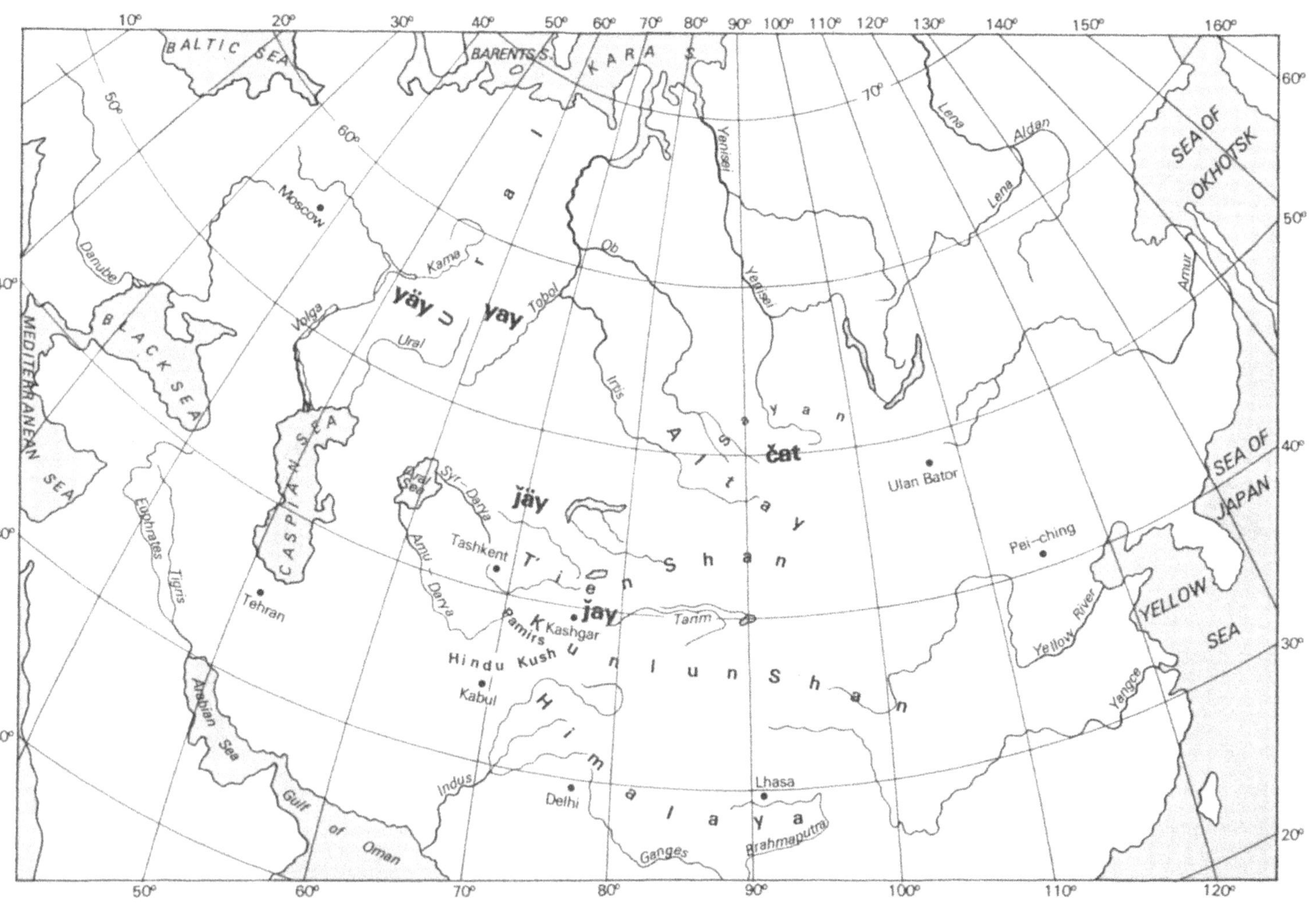
BALTIC SEA
BARENTS S.
KARA S.
SEA OF OKHOTSK
SEA OF JAPAN
YELLOW SEA
MEDITERRANEAN SEA
BLACK SEA
CASPIAN SEA
Aral Sea
Arabian Sea
Gulf of Oman
Moscow
Tehran
Tashkent
Kashgar
Kabul
Delhi
Lhasa
Ulan Bator
Pei-ching
Danube
Volga
Kama
Ural
Tobol
Ob
Irtis
Yenisei
Lena
Aldan
Amur
Syr-Darya
Amu-Darya
Euphrates
Tigris
Indus
Ganges
Brahmaputra
Tarim
Yellow River
Yangce
Ural
Sayan
Altay
T'ien Shan
Pamirs
Hindu Kush
Kunlun Shan
Himalaya
yäy ⊃ yay
jäy
jay
čat
10°
20°
30°
40°
50°
60°
70°
80°
90°
100°
110°
120°
130°
140°
150°
160°

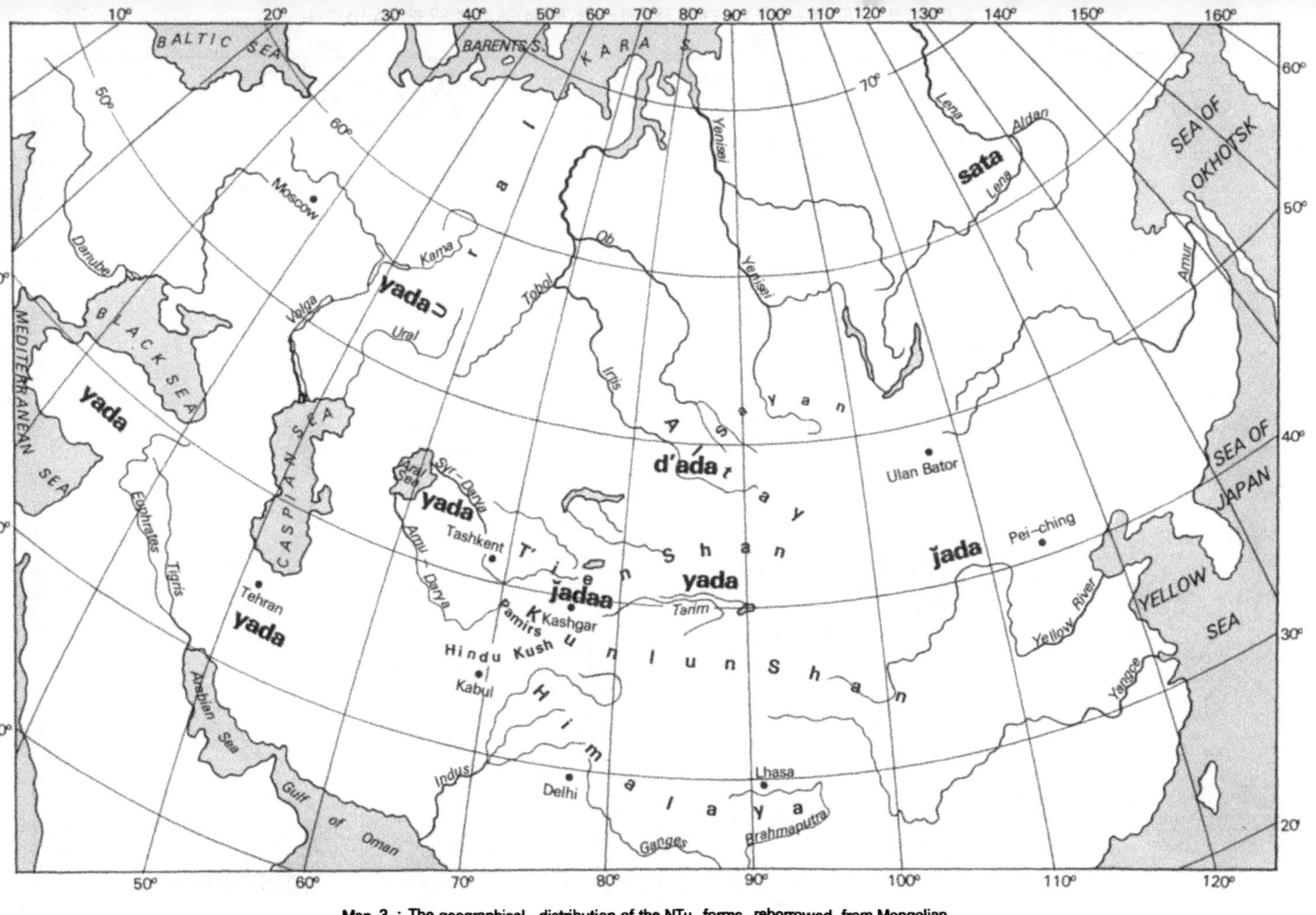

Map 3. : The geographical distribution of the NTu. forms reborrowed from Mongolian

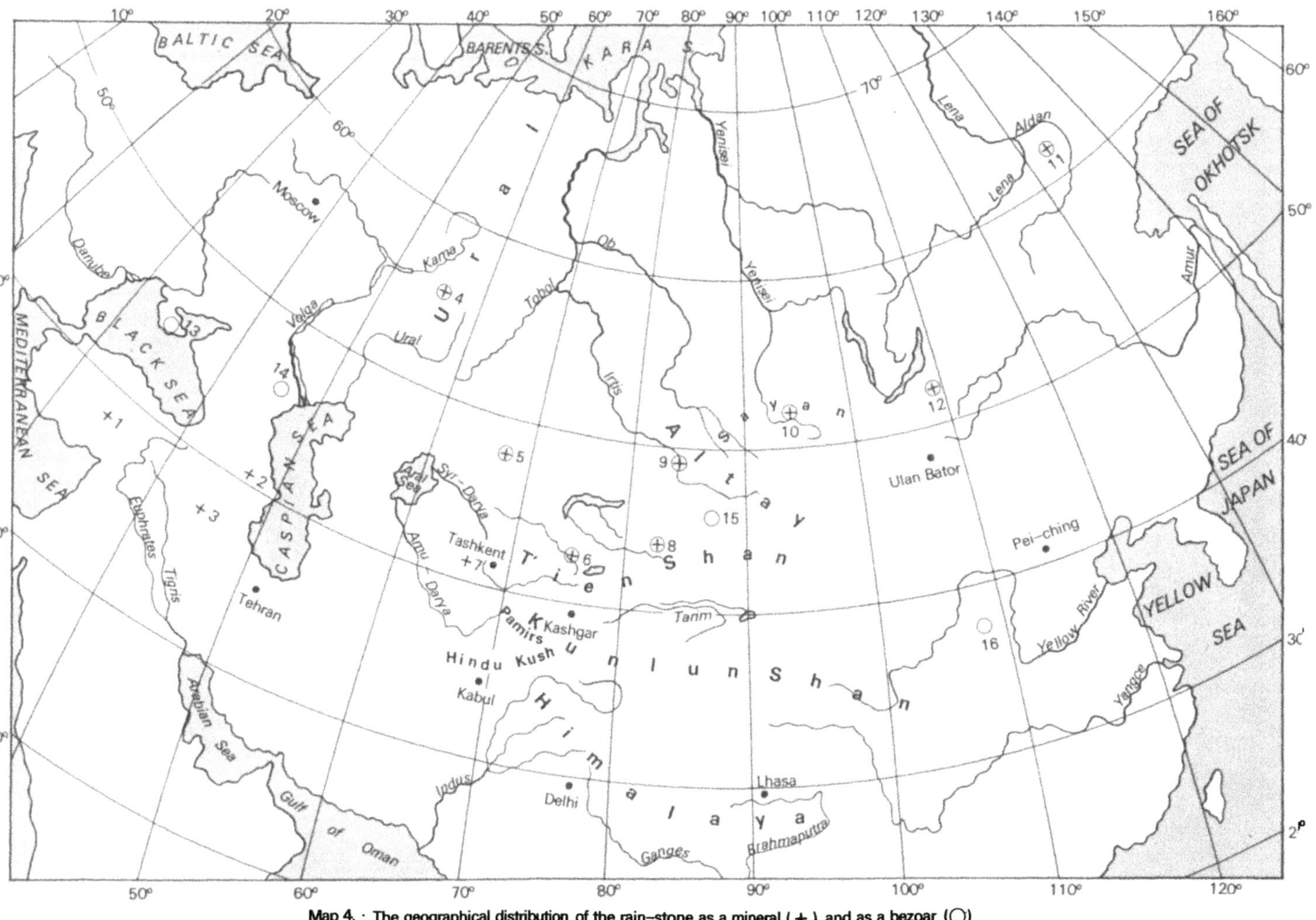

Map 4. : The geographical distribution of the rain-stone as a mineral (+) and as a bezoar (◯)

www.ingramcontent.com/pod-product-compliance
Lightning Source LLC
Chambersburg PA
CBHW021540260326
41914CB00001B/98

* 9 7 8 0 9 3 3 0 7 0 3 3 2 *